An Introduction to

Archaeology

David Miles

A Hyperion Book
Ward Lock Limited · London

© David Miles 1978

A Hyperion Book

First published in Great Britain in 1978
in association with Peter Crawley
by Ward Lock Limited, 116 Baker Street,
London, W1M 2BB, a member of the Pentos Group.

Layout by Paul Turner

Printed and bound by
Cox & Wyman Ltd, London, Fakenham and Reading

British Library Cataloguing in Publication Data

Miles, David
   An introduction to archaeology.
   1. Archaeology—Great Britain
   I. Title
   936.1   CC101.G7

ISBN 0–7063–5725–6

Contents

Acknowledgments

In a book like *An Introduction to Archaeology* an author is totally dependent on the work of many fellow students. I would firstly like to thank all those archaeologists, only some of whom are mentioned in the text and bibliography, on whose efforts I have drawn. For their generous help with illustrations and general advice I must mention Tom Hassall, Trevor Rowley, Martin Welch of the Ashmolean Museum, the staff of the Cambridge University Department of Aerial Photography, in particular Rowan Whimster, and Alan Aberg of the National Monuments Record. Professor Keith Branigan kindly read the text, and I am grateful for his comments. All the drawings are the work of Wendy Lee. I am particularly indebted to Sue Unstead and Deborah Wakeling of Ward Lock Limited for their help on the manuscript, and finally I must thank my wife, Gwyn, without whose encouragement, patience and criticism this book would not have been written.

Thanks are also due to the following museums, collections and photographers by whose courtesy the illustrations in the book are reproduced:
Ashmolean Museum, University of Oxford 16, 28 *top*, 29, 30 *bottom*, 41, 47, 62, 70, 78 *bottom*, 81
Author's Collection 8, 9 *top*, 64 *left*, 94 *both*, *jacket*
J. Bailey 65
P. Barker 102 *top*
British Museum 79 *both*
Cambridge University Collection 17, 28 *bottom*, 33, 34, 42, 50 *top*, 57 *top*, 72 *top*, 73, 87, 109
D. Carpenter 97
T. Champion 74
John Coles 39 *bottom*, 40
Department of the Environment (Crown Copyright) 36, 39 *top*, 50 *bottom*, 61 *top*
P. Dixon 46 *bottom*
Mike S. Duffy 58
Trevor Hurst 60
W. T. Jones 10
Lincoln Excavation Committee 53 *top*
Museum of London (Department of Urban Archaeology) 60, 65
National Monuments Record (Crown Copyright) 69 *bottom*, 76
Oxford Archaeological Unit 97
Oxford Excavation Committee 20 *top*, 63
Oxfordshire Department of Museums Services 95
P. J. Reynolds 108 *top*
A. Saville 109 *top and centre left*
R. F. Smith 102 *bottom*
University of Southampton (Department of Archaeology) 74
York Archaeological Trust 58

Introduction

Towering piles of leaden cloud wallow around the Thames Valley. To the south lightning flickers over the beech-capped downland of Wittenham Clumps. On a rainswept gravel pit a team of archaeologists crouch over newly discovered graves. They scrape off sandy soil to reveal the hard, clean bones of men and women who died 1,500 years ago. As the damp earth is trowelled away, iron spears, knives, belt buckles and shield bosses gradually become visible alongside the skeletons of these earliest Englishmen. Amber beads and gilded brooches with abstract, convoluted decoration adorn the women.

Paganissimi: Bede had called these people 'very pagan', and like good pagans, in death they carry the symbols of their status in life. But their resurrection is witnessed not only by a few blasé archaeologists; a constant stream of excited visitors look on. 'How do you know where to dig?' 'Aren't their teeth good?' 'Can you tell what they died of?' 'How old are they?' The questions come fast and furious and are familiar to any archaeologist.

In 1771 an early antiquary, Bryan Fausset, who suffered from gout, began his excavations at the crack of dawn because 'I know myself liable to be pestered with a numerous set of troublesome spectators'. In two hours his labourers dug through nine barrows, and he was able to return to his breakfast undisturbed by any curious onlookers. Two centuries later Sir Mortimer Wheeler, the doyen of British archaeology, took a different attitude: 'I was, and am, convinced of the moral and academic necessity of sharing scientific work to the fullest possible extent with the man in the street and in the field. Today . . . he is in fact our employer.' Wheeler was right: one of the strengths of British archaeology is the interest it arouses in so many people. Reports of our bleak Thames-side cemetery appeared in local newspapers and *The Times*, on radio and TV. In spite of the weather, crowds turned up in droves, fascinated to see how archaeologists work and to share the excitement of uncovering the past.

Whenever archaeological excavations appear in the news, we hear words like 'the oldest', 'the richest', 'the most important' and other superlatives. Archaeologists seem to be glorified treasure-hunters, looking for spectacular remains and disappointed if they do not find them. Or they are working around the clock, desperately rescuing some Roman mosaic from the maw of an insatiable bulldozer. These stereotyped romantic images are not entirely

7

true: archaeology is more than a 'popular opiate', and the reality is no less interesting.

To understand the study of the past we need to consider briefly what archaeologists think archaeology is, not that you will ever find two who will agree with each other. Most will almost certainly disagree with the *Shorter Oxford English Dictionary* definitions 'Ancient history generally; systematic description or study of antiquities' or 'The scientific study of the remains and monuments of the prehistoric period.' Archaeology is concerned with the systematic study of the material remains of human communities—the surviving structures, pottery, tools and general debris that people in the past have left behind them. It differs from history in the narrow sense in that it does not rely on written evidence. Archaeology is not solely concerned, though, with 'prehistoric' periods. 'Prehistoric' means, literally, before the use of writing. *Homo sapiens*, as we modestly call ourselves, and our ancestors have been around for about two million years. Writing appeared in the Near East little more than 5,000 years ago. It is less than 2,000 years since the first documents were written in Britain, and in vast areas of the world—Africa, America and Australia—writing is an even more recent innovation.

Berinsfield, Oxfordshire: the excavation of a pagan Saxon cemetery found during gravel extraction. The bones are well preserved in the alkaline soil.

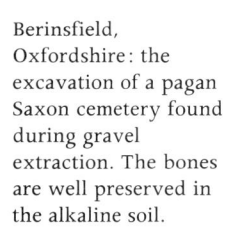

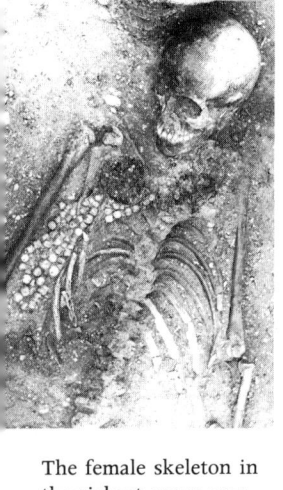

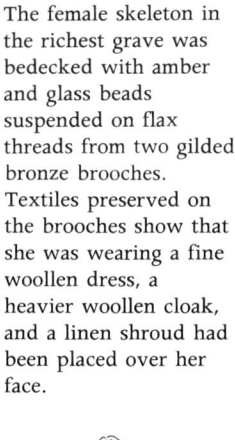

The female skeleton in the richest grave was bedecked with amber and glass beads suspended on flax threads from two gilded bronze brooches. Textiles preserved on the brooches show that she was wearing a fine woollen dress, a heavier woollen cloak, and a linen shroud had been placed over her face.

Archaeology enables us to find out about people who existed long before the invention of writing or before its introduction into their particular society. On the other hand, archaeology is not solely concerned with pre-historic peoples. Britain was the northern outpost of the Roman world for over 300 years and part of an extremely literate empire. Yet there are many aspects of life in Roman Britain about which history tells us very little. Caesar describes his temporary conquests and a little about the local inhabitants. We hear about the activities of Agricola, Governor of Britain between AD 78 and 84, from his son-in-law Tacitus; we have road maps and military, civic and religious inscriptions but only one mention in passing of a Romano-British villa; we have no account of local laws or methods of agriculture, land-holding, the size and health of the population, communities outside the towns; and we know very little about the economy of Roman Britain. Even in medieval England there are aspects of life about which historical documents tell us very little. So archaeology is useful even in the study of literate, historic societies, and many people, of course, particularly in Africa and America, remained 'prehistoric' until they emerged into the glare of the twentieth century.

Every newly elected professor of archaeology faced with the inevitable inaugural lecture has felt it necessary to define his subject. There have been many variations of emphasis, but most are agreed in principle with Professor Grahame Clark that it is the 'systematic study of antiquities as a means of reconstructing the past'. The archaeologist cannot question the occupants of an ancient settlement in person; he cannot ask them how they earn their livelihood, what sort of houses they live in, how many people occupy each one; he cannot watch them at mealtimes to see what sort of food they eat, attend their religious festivals and funerals or listen to their speech and music. But the archaeologist can look at the present-day landscape to find traces of most of these things and he can attempt to put together a map of the landscape at different periods. Like an electrician looking at a circuit diagram, the archaeologist can begin to see how ancient societies fit together and operate.

Excavation enables the archaeologist to examine the scene of the crime. Thousands of pieces of evidence are uncovered and, as Professor Clark emphasized, *systematically* examined. The principles are not difficult to grasp because we make similar judgments in our everyday lives. Although verbal communication is obviously important, visual impressions make even more impact. We get a fairly good idea of a man's status from his physical appearance, what he wears and what sort of car he drives. We may be able to predict his job, especially if he is wearing a uniform, what sort of house he lives in or even how he might vote. Most of us, when we enter a strange house, are able to say something about the occupants.

We do not all have the luck or the inspiration of Sherlock Holmes, but everyone is capable of making assessments about people from purely physical

evidence. We will not always be right but in the normal course of our lives we often make deductions and inferences on this basis. The archaeologist is in the position of the person entering a strange room, with a slight disadvantage, after the occupants have moved out. They may have left behind a certain amount of debris, but even this may not survive. In most circumstances organic material quickly perishes. Textiles, wood and leather are only found in exceptionally wet or dry conditions. Even human bones can disappear in an acidic soil.

The room in which I am writing contains hundreds of items of evidence. Any visitor would have little difficulty in guessing my occupation or interests, the number of people who use the study, their age and sex. But if, like the ashes of Vesuvius settling on Pliny in Pompeii, the Cotswolds were to rain down on my head, would the picture be so clear for a future archaeologist? By far the best evidence, the books around the walls, would rapidly disappear, and the carpets and curtains along with them. I am afraid the coats hanging on the back of the door, which say so much about the room's occupants, would not last for long. The wood and leather-topped desk at which I am writing would disappear except for its brass handles. There would be other clues.

Saxon burial at Mucking, Essex. In the acidic gravel of this site only a silhouette of the skeleton remains.

On the desk top are three pots in which I keep pencils, plastic pens and rulers. Plastic and well-fired pottery is practically indestructible. One of the pots might complicate the picture a little for our future archaeologist because it was made in Africa in the nineteenth century; so might the Eskimo soapstone carving beside it. There is a plastic and metal typewriter on the desk and there are several boxes of colour slides in plastic mounts. On a shelf above there is a human skull belonging to a lady who lived in the Orkney Islands 1,000 years ago—I dug her up myself. There are two cameras sitting alongside her and a balalaika brought back from a trip to Russia. And then, of course, there is me.

In the local lime-rich soils human bone is preserved indefinitely. It would provide the evidence for a male in his late twenties with, even if I say so myself, few obvious physical defects. Clothes would not survive except for the buttons on my shirt and a belt buckle, also a watch and a pair of spectacles. The archaeologist would no doubt be delighted to find lying near my right hip four coins. They are all tenpenny pieces decorated with the head of Queen Elizabeth II. One of them has the date 1965 on it, another 1969, and the remaining two were both minted in 1976. The archaeologist would not assume our catastrophe occurred in 1976; instead he would say that this particular site was occupied until 1976 or later. The coins, in spite of rubbing around in my pocket, are not very worn, so they have not been in circulation long. It is the colours, furnishings, the books and the pictures on the walls which give the room its character. These would disappear shortly after our hypothetical disaster, but the surviving evidence would provide a rich vein of information, and if archaeologists in the future do their job as well as I trust they will, they should recognize in these material remains the presence of one of their own primitive ancestors.

1 Attitudes to the past

Man is a curious animal and has always speculated about his own past. These speculations have taken the form of myths and legends, shown through sagas, poetry, dances, paintings and sculpture, or bombastic propaganda to support a ruling house. Archaeology, the systematic and objective study of the material remains of the past, is a relatively youthful subject. To understand modern archaeology it is necessary to examine man's changing attitude to the past and the development of archaeology as a scientific subject.

Over 2,500 years ago Nabonidus, King of Babylon, ordered holes to be dug into the ruins of the ancient city of Ur. He recovered objects which were ancient even then, and his daughter Beshalti-Nanner kept the collection in a special room. Thucydides, writing in Athens in the fifth century BC, was intellectually light-years ahead of the Babylonians. He wanted to describe and explain the past and convey his ideas to his fellow men. In his account of the Peloponnesian Wars he tells us that some old graves at Delos had been opened. The Athenians assumed from the method of burial and the accompanying weapons that these were the graves of Carians. Thucydides did not make the leap from this deduction to appreciating the possibilities of archaeology as a means of reconstructing the past; neither did the medieval monks who, while robbing stone from the ruins of the Roman town of Verulamium (St Albans), found Roman pottery, glass and inscriptions.

Fellow monks at Abingdon recorded in a thirteenth-century chronicle the discovery of a small pin, decorated with a cross inside a circle. To them this became the Black Cross of Abingdon, a revered relic supposedly made from a nail of the True Cross and brought to the nearby nunnery of St Helen. We can see from the description and illustration in the chronicle that the monks had, in fact, found what archaeologists now call a disc-headed pin. These pins have been discovered in modern excavations on other monastic sites and date to the seventh century. The pin supports the tradition that the nunnery was founded in the seventh century, but to the medieval monks it provided an excuse to glamorize the past, to forge a link with St Helen, mother of Constantine the Great and finder of the True Cross, and Jesus Christ all in one fell swoop.

Medieval monks appreciated the worldly fact that the past is powerful: it bestows respectability, establishes credentials and the right to authority.

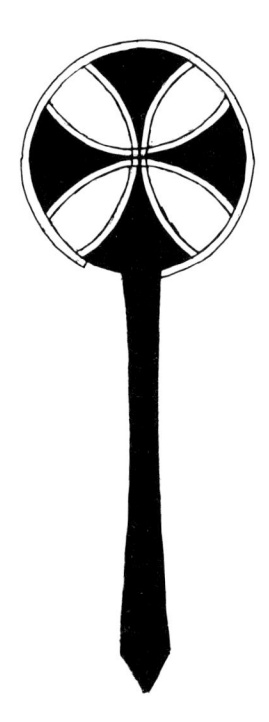

The illustration of the Black Cross of Abingdon taken from a 13th-century chronicle of Abingdon Abbey. The medieval monks who dug it up believed it to be made from a nail of the True Cross, but archaeologists now recognize it as a 7th-century pin.

12

The monks invented a panoply of pseudo-historical characters to increase the status of their establishments, none more so than the public-relations experts of Glastonbury Abbey, who had nothing to learn from the owners of our commercialized stately homes. Joseph of Arimathea, the youthful Jesus, St Patrick, St Dunstan and Gildas were all linked with Glastonbury Abbey, making it the oldest and holiest Christian establishment in England. The old propaganda retains its potency: in the late 60s crowds of hippies trailed around the site 'to feel the vibrations', much to the annoyance of unsympathetic townsfolk.

In the Middle Ages the dominance of the Church and biblical authority sustained an overwhelming spirit of unenquiry. But if human history was ultimately unimportant in the face of God's ordinance, the past could still be used and manipulated. National pride and ruling dynasties required pedigrees worthy of a Cruft's champion: biblical and Classical forefathers were essential. Geoffrey of Monmouth's *Historia Regum Britanniae*, written, probably at Oxford, about 1135, provided such a past for the newly emergent Norman Kingdom of England with devastating effect. As T. D. Kendrick said in his great survey *British Antiquity* (1950), 'Within fifteen years of its publication not to have read it was a matter of reproach . . . it swept away opposition with the ruthless force of a great epic.' Geoffrey conjured up Brutus the Trojan, who founded London, King Lear, King Cole of Colchester, Belinus, the builder of Billingsgate, Merlin, who moved Stonehenge from Ireland to Wiltshire, and Arthur, a general of Napoleonic proportions. His characters lodged themselves in the national consciousness with the persistence of fish-hooks and have hardly been withdrawn from popular mythology even today. Kendrick hit the nail on the head: Geoffrey of Monmouth had produced 'an irresistibly good book in an age when such works were very rare'.

Until the mid-fifteenth century the Trojan origin of the British was hardly doubted. Even William of Worcester (1415–82), author of the *Itinerarium*, did not question Geoffrey's view, although he took a serious interest in the visible traces of monuments, then ancient and modern, and his survey of Bristol is probably the first great work of British topography.

In the fifteenth century on the Continent a more rational approach was developing towards nationalist fables. England, however, gained a new dynasty, the Tudors, which was much in need of the old mythology. Geoffrey of Monmouth's stories of Celtic heroes cast a cosy glow of legitimacy over the new Welsh royal family, and Henry Tudor, basking in the reflected aura, named his first son Arthur.

The first cracks in the fossilized thinking of medieval Europe appeared in Italy. The great explosion of creativity which we call the Renaissance brought with it new attitudes towards the study of the past, spreading out like ripples from Venice, Florence, Milan and Ferrara to France, Germany and northern Europe. Men like Leonardo da Vinci were polymaths, tackling architecture and engineering, biology and physics, painting and sculpture with equal

vigour. The tremendous interest in Latin texts, revived by Dante, Petrarch and Boccaccio, gave a fresh historical perspective. And this at a time when the great voyages of discovery were reminding Europeans that there were other infinitely varied human societies around the world.

The study of Classical writers reminded European man that he had not sprung fully armed like Athena from the head of Zeus. Lucretius in the first century BC said: 'Hands, tooth and nail and stones were the ancient weapons; branches ripped from forests, flames and fire, once they were known. Later the force of iron and bronze was discovered; the use of bronze was learnt before iron . . . The naked and unarmed surrendered to those equipped with weapons. Gradually the iron sword came to the fore, the bronze sickle was scorned, and they began to plough up the soil of the earth with iron.'

Renaissance scholars were able to make the conceptual leap from just reading these Roman and Greek folk memories to actually seeking physical evidence for themselves. Michele Mercati (1541–93), superintendent of the Vatican's botanical gardens, combined the study of ancient authorities and the collection of ethnographic objects from America and Asia with field-work in order to explain the stone tools which he found in the soil of Italy. He recognized flint arrowheads and axes for what they were, not simply the fairy stones of popular superstition. Mercati's three-pronged approach of documentary study, ethnography and field observation formed the basis of modern archaeology, and although his *Metallotheca Vaticana* was not published until 1717, his attitude to the problems of the past gradually penetrated the rest of Europe.

Ironically, England's Renaissance prince, Henry VIII, encouraged the study of antiquities while dissolving the main repositories of historical knowledge, the monasteries. Henry employed a royal commissioner, John Leland (c. 1506–52), to seek out ancient manuscripts, many of which were not so much safeguarded in monasteries as decomposing and neglected there. Leland was learned, fanatically patriotic, irascible, and eventually went mad. In his prime he was fascinated by everything around him and not given to romanticizing. Consequently, the factual descriptions in his *Itinerary* remain a mine of information. The Elizabethan antiquary, William Camden (1551–1623), also adopted a rational attitude, defending his subject from its critics: 'In the study of Antiquity there is a sweet food in the mind well befitting such as are of honest and noble disposition.' Camden's *Britannia* contained the first English archaeological illustrations, appropriately one of Stonehenge and drawings of British coins.

In the seventeenth century the study of antiquity did not exactly gain acceptance in England. John Milton spoke for more than himself when he sneered at those 'who take pleasure to be all their lifetimes raking the foundations of old abbeys and cathedrals'. John Aubrey, best known nowadays for his delightful, gossipy *Brief Lives*, seems unusually pathetic when he writes: 'This searching after Antiquities is a wearisome taske . . . for nobody els

hereabouts hardly cares for it, but rather makes a scorn of it.' Yet Aubrey was himself one of the greatest observers of antiquities, and his *Monumenta Britannica* was, for its time, a model of objective description. Like the botanist John Ray, Aubrey was one of the 'New Men' of the mid-seventeenth century, an advocate of the cardinal rules of Francis Bacon: observation, experimentation, recording and classification. County surveys and natural histories appeared which were all-embracing and essentially practical. Robert Plot's *Natural History of Oxfordshire* (1677) is typical of the genre, listing the region's natural resources but with a strong emphasis on antiquities.

This was the heyday of collectors, accumulators of the fantastic and the curious, things geological, archaeological and natural historical: specialization was not in fashion. Ole Worm in Copenhagen and the Tradescants in London laid the foundations for the great museums of the present day. John Tradescant, gardener to Queen Henrietta Maria, formed a collection of 'varieties and oddities', popularly known as Tradescant's Ark. Eventually bequeathed to Oxford University, this formed the nucleus of the Ashmolean Museum. Individuals like Sir Thomas Browne (1605–82) with his 'vast curiosity' surrounded themselves with a bewildering array of objects which, in spite of their dilettante appearance, provided the raw material for direct observation and experimentation. Herman Melville, author of *Moby Dick*, turned to Browne's sonorous prose for descriptions of whales, and archaeologists recognize him as the author of the first excavation report. His versatility was typical of the later seventeenth century in England.

Ole Worm's Museum in Copenhagen complete with weapons, costumes, shells, rocks and assorted beasts, a 17th-century cabinet of curiosities which laid the foundations for modern museums.

A view of Stonehenge by William Turner of Oxford (1789–1851). In this early 19th-century watercolour Salisbury Plain is still grazed by sheep and Stonehenge stands at the centre of a cluster of burial mounds unravaged by prairie farmers, tourists or traffic.

The study of antiquity failed to rise beyond its curiosity value. Dr Johnson, Thomas Browne's biographer, in spite of his admiration for the man as a writer who made the past 'like coloured fireworks burn', failed to see any significance in his study of ancient burial customs. In the hundred years, or more, following the 'New Men' antiquarianism deteriorated into Gothic Romanticism and treasure-hunting. The decline can be seen in an individual, William Stukeley (1687–1765). With the combined skills of a country land-agent, surveyor and acute observer, Stukeley's early work established him as one of the fathers of the field-work tradition in British archaeology. Born in 1687, Stukeley lived at a time of increasing mobility and greater communications. He was an admirer of Newton, Ray and Aubrey, and on horseback he visited sites as far afield as Avebury, Stonehenge and Hadrian's Wall. But times were changing, and Stukeley reflected his times. In 1729 he abandoned his chosen profession, medicine, for the Church. Like the national mood, his own shifted from the Rational to the Romantic. Antiquities became more popular than ever but steeped in a cloying atmosphere of irrational emotion and mysticism. The good sense of Camden was swamped by a host of morbid Druids clad in white sheets, waving sickles and mistletoe.

It is perhaps unfortunate that the popularity of excavation grew at the same time as the Romantic movement. As a consequence throughout the nineteenth century digging was little more than a field sport, and barrows were bagged in almost as large a quantity as grouse. Dean Meriwether may have set some kind of record when in 1849 he 'did' thirty-five barrows on the Marlborough Downs of Wiltshire in twenty-eight days. The newly

16

Housesteads, one of the finest forts on Hadrian's Wall. The military garrison attracted traders and a settlement grew up around it, now visible as earthworks and preserved beneath the turf.

founded and long-winded British Archaeological Association for the Encouragement and Prosecution of Researches into the Arts and Monuments of the Early Middle Ages held the first-ever archaeological conference at Canterbury in 1844. The entertainment included tours of the cathedral, displays, the unwrapping of an Egyptian mummy and the opening of eight barrows on Breach Down. Two hundred guests watched from their carriages, while Lord Albert Conyngham supervised the excavation 'dressed in an exploring costume'. Not surprisingly some voices were raised in protest against those who desecrated 'time-hallowed monuments for no better purpose than the indulgence of craving acquisitiveness and the adorning of glass cases with ill-understood relics'.

Very gradually excavation techniques improved, most notably at the end of the century with the systematically organized, military-style operations of General Pitt-Rivers (1827–1900). His excavations on Cranborne Chase in Wiltshire were meticulous and objective. Everything was recorded, not simply the spectacular, and Pitt-Rivers consciously attempted to eliminate personal bias from what he considered should be a scientific activity.

Pitt-Rivers dragged archaeological technique into the twentieth century, but more important was the tremendous conceptual shift which had taken place in the preceding fifty years. The work of Continental prehistorians, the results of the increasingly professional science of geology and the revolutionary ideas of Darwin shattered the rigid shell which had enclosed and fossilized the European concept of time. Until that breakthrough archaeology was bound within a sterile strait-jacket.

2 Dating the past

'The poor world is almost six thousand years old', said Rosalind in *As You Like It*. With current estimates of five billion years for the age of the world, Shakespeare's earth seems to us a mere youngster. In the seventeenth century Shakespeare had to rely on the estimates of Archbishop Usher of Armagh who calculated from the book of Genesis that the world was created in 4004 BC With staggering confidence Dr John Lightfoot (1602–75), Vice-Chancellor of Cambridge University, proposed a more precise moment of creation, 23 October 4004 BC at 9.00 a.m., appropriately convenient, as Professor Glyn Daniel has pointed out, for the start of his university's term. The date of 4004 BC was sufficiently accepted to be printed in the margin of the Authorized Version of the Bible. Such dogmatism on the part of the Church proved to be a serious handicap to the developing study of the past, and overwhelming evidence had to be amassed before this time barrier was smashed.

To begin to understand the past the archaeologist must be able to order his evidence along a time-scale either to assign an absolute date, like Usher's 4004 BC, or a relative one, such as A is older than B which is older than C. In the seventeenth century all human history had to be fitted into a mere 6,000 years. The Roman Empire, the civilization of Greece, the rule of the Pharaohs in Egypt and the biblical adventures of the Israelites were almost sufficient in themselves to fill the known span of mankind. Historical evidence alone could account for the whole of man's time on earth, at least if he lived around the Mediterranean. In Britain there were still 4,000 years of prehistory to explain but, as we have seen, this was done by conjuring up the wraiths of the Great British myth.

Imposing structures such as Stonehenge or the Megalithic tomb of New Grange in Ireland were usually seen as the work of Phoenicians, Egyptians, Druids or some other stock historical characters. Only a few people speculated in theoretical terms of 'hunting communities' or 'early farmers' who might not exist in the historical record but might, nevertheless, have played a part in the formation of human society. The group of men now known as the Scottish Primitivists attempted to think along these lines but met with scorn and derision. When Samuel Johnson said of such ideas 'Sir, it is all conjecture about a thing useless, even if it were known to be true', he reflected the

general feeling that the human past was only to be found in written records and nothing else was of interest.

In *The Idea of Prehistory* (1962) Glyn Daniel has pointed out the prevailing pessimism amongst antiquaries in the early nineteenth century. A breakthrough in the time barrier seemed impossible to Professor Rasmus Nyerup of Copenhagen University when he said 'everything which has come down to us from heathendom is wrapped in a thick fog; it belongs to a space of time which we cannot measure. We know that it is older than Christendom but whether by a couple of years or a couple of centuries, or even by more than a millennium, we can do no more than guess.'

Yet the fog was about to be blown away: geologists were in the process of discovering fossils of extinct species of animals and beginning to understand the principles of stratigraphy. The appearance of Sir Charles Lyell's *Principles of Geology* (1830–3) put several nails into the coffin of the biblical fundamentalists and laid the foundation for the ideas of Darwin. According to Lyell, the earth had not been created a neat, immutable whole but had evolved subject to forces which were still in evidence, and the process had been a very slow one.

The realization that human fossils and man-made tools occurred in association with the fossils of extinct animals was accepted by many people only with great difficulty. The old preconceptions died hard, but in 1859 twenty years of research by Jacques Boucher de Crèvecoeur de Perthes, a customs official of Abbeville in the Somme Valley, were rewarded. His discoveries of flint tools along with the bones of elephant and rhinoceros deep within the Somme gravels were described at the Society of Antiquaries in London. His conclusion that man's history could not be encompassed within a mere 6,000 years was generally accepted, at least in academic circles.

The evidence for the antiquity of man depended on a principle first emphasized by geologists, that of stratification. Like most good ideas it is quite a simple one. Geologists realized that where they found layers of rock superimposed upon one another those near the surface were the most recent and the deeper ones became progressively older. There could be exceptions to the general rule when, for example, there had been movements in the earth's crust as a result of seismic activity. Then the strata could be folded and bent or even turned upside down, but careful observation enabled geologists to detect such anomalies.

The principle of stratification applies in archaeological excavation. Human occupation on one site over many generations can result in the deposition of many metres of debris. In the Middle East there are artificial mounds, or tells, which may be 30 m high. They are formed by the successive construction and demolition of clay-brick buildings in settlements which have been occupied for 4,000 years or more. Jericho or Heinrich Schliemann's Troy are such sites, and as excavation continues downward, older and older layers are reached.

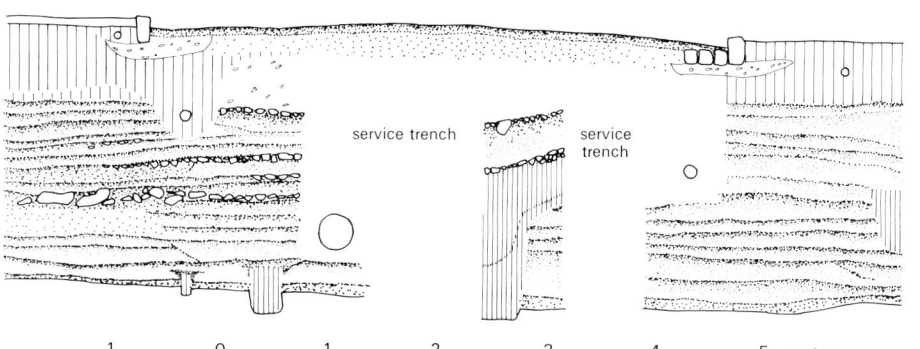

Castle Street, Oxford. During the redevelopment of the St Ebbe's area of the city a section was cut across this street. Beneath the modern tarmac are seventeen earlier street surfaces dating back to late Saxon times.

service trench   service trench

1   0   1   2   3   4   5   metres

In Britain cities like London, Lincoln or Winchester do not look like obvious mounds, yet their streets are often several metres above those of the underlying medieval and Roman towns as a result of the build-up of 2,000 years of human debris. This is particularly true in low-lying places like York and Dublin where a high water-table encouraged Roman, Viking and medieval townspeople to build on the rubbish of their predecessors in order to keep above the damp.

Urban sites are extremely complex, and although the principle of stratigraphy holds good, it should not be assumed that deeper always means older. Medieval town-dwellers were extremely industrious diggers of pits, mainly in order to dispose of their refuse, and might go down several metres through the underlying strata. As a result archaeologists can find pottery of, say, the fourteenth century well below the level of a Roman building built 100 years after Christ.

20

Stratigraphy in itself does not provide a date for an archaeological feature such as a pit. What it does do is enable the archaeologist to sort the layers of the site into the correct order. Within the deposits are often found material remains of human activity. There may be flint tools, pottery, metalwork, animal bones or traces of plants utilized by man. Occasionally the discovery of coins or inscriptions may give an obvious clue to the date of a particular layer, but most objects are less vocal than coins. It is more difficult to assess the age of a flint axe, a bronze dagger or an iron knife.

In spite of Rasmus Nyerup's despair early in the nineteenth century when faced with the amorphous collection of ancient artefacts in the Museum at Copenhagen, his successor, Christian Thomsen (1788–1865), made a breakthrough which is still fundamental to archaeological thinking. Thomsen imposed order where previously chaos had existed when he classified his material into Stone, Bronze and Iron. The idea of Three Ages of material technology was not new—even ancient Greek writers, like Hesiod, and Renaissance Italian antiquaries had mentioned it. Thomsen's guide to the National Museum, produced in 1836, formalized the Three Age System, and to him goes the credit for creating a three-dimensional image of man's past. Opposition to Thomsen's largely theoretical scheme was soon overcome by discoveries in excavations of stratified material which fitted the sequence he had proposed.

Thomsen's Three Age System did not put actual dates on prehistoric periods but it did provide a framework into which material and sites could be placed. Sir John Lubbock (1834–1913) in his best-selling *Prehistoric Times*, published in 1865, further divided the Stone Age into Palaeolithic and Neolithic or Old and New Stone Age. He differentiated between the earliest period when stone tools were chipped into shape and the later phase of polished flint tools. The Three Age System has weathered many criticisms and is undoubtedly a gross simplification. Nevertheless, it is still widely used, and only in recent years, with the refinement provided by scientific dating techniques, have some prehistorians begun, very gradually, to dispense with it.

In northern Europe documented history began with the Roman invasions in the years before and after the birth of Christ. Stratigraphy and theoretical systems like the Three Ages suggested that prehistory must extend back many thousand years, but there were no historical events on which to hang the relative sequences. The solution to this problem came by finding associations between Europe and the literate south. In Egypt accurate historical calendars extend back to about 3000 BC, records conscientiously kept on behalf of kings jealous of their pedigrees. As a result archaeological objects excavated in Egypt can be dated very accurately when found in tombs or buildings associated with historical records.

Sir Flinders Petrie (1853–1942) forged the first links between prehistoric Europe and Egypt when, in 1891, he spotted Egyptian objects at Mycenae in southern Greece. He was able to date them and, consequently, a phase at

The development of flint technology: Palaeolithic flaked flint handaxe (below), and late Neolithic polished flint axe (above).

Mycenae to about 1500 BC. This method of cross-dating subsequently proved to be very successful and enabled students of Aegean archaeology to date the palace civilization of Crete and Greek Bronze Age sites such as Mycenae and Tiryns.

The inevitable dependence on Egyptian links to establish a chronology for southern Europe encouraged a narrow view of European prehistory in general. 'Diffusionism' was the tendency to see all major developments in barbarian Europe as dependent on the influence of Egypt or some other part of the eastern Mediterranean world. Professor Gordon Childe (1892–1957) described the growth of European prehistoric cultures as 'the irradiation of European barbarism by Oriental civilization'. He was largely adopting the views of the Swede, Oscar Montelius (1843–1921), who in 1899 wrote *Der Orient und Europa* (The Orient and Europe), a book that has been called 'the first coherent view of European prehistory'. Two basic themes underpinned Montelius' great work. The first was his belief that Oriental ideas diffused into Europe a sort of cultural imperialism and that artefacts reflecting this influence could be found in Europe and used for cross-dating purposes. The second theory was that objects could be classified on typological grounds to provide a relative sequence of dating.

Since Montelius, the construction of typologies has been a favourite pastime of archaeologists. The theory is probably easiest to understand if we think of modern automobiles. There is a fairly clear development from a Model T Ford of the 20s through a 50s' Ford Popular to a Ford Cortina of the 60s. You do not have to be much of an autophile to spot the evolution of style in cars or, in terms of fashion, to put the bustle, the New Look and the miniskirt in the right order. Montelius' typologies worked on the same principle of slotting a series of similar objects, such as daggers, axes, pots or brooches, into the correct order. Simple in theory but difficult in practice, it depends on the archaeologist's identifying technological developments and modifications and putting them in the correct sequence. Of course, things do not necessarily evolve as logically as we like to think. Nevertheless, it is an essential dating method, and a proposed sequence of objects can be tested against the results of excavation until a convincing typology emerges.

The evolution of a pottery style. These black-burnished vessels were made by Durotrigan potters in south-west Britain: *left c.* AD 40; *centre* 2nd century AD; *right* late 3rd or 4th century AD.

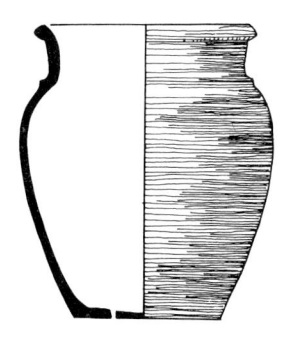
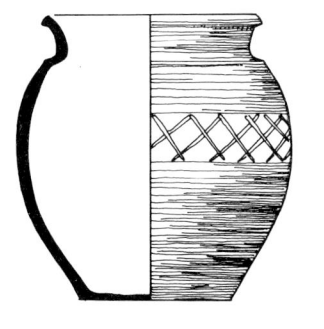
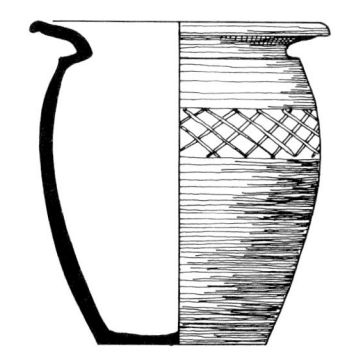

Archaeology in the first half of the twentieth century was dominated by diffusionist thinking. It could result in the meticulous network of inter-relationships built up by Montelius and later by Gordon Childe in *The Dawn of European Civilisation* (1925) or, at the opposite end of the spectrum, the extreme diffusionist stance of Elliot Grafton Smith (1871–1937). For Smith, Egypt was the birthplace of everything, literally. When asked what was happening in the rest of the world while Egypt was creating the basis of civilization, he answered quite simply: 'Nothing.' Even today the lunatic fringe of archaeology is alive and well; Elliot Grafton Smith's disciples can still occasionally be sighted, sailing across some ocean in a paper boat pursued by TV cameras.

The Egyptian connection provided a convincing chronology for the Aegean area, if only as far back as 3000 BC. Before that was largely guesswork. Even after 3000 BC Egyptian objects were not found beyond Greece: the rest of Europe could not be directly linked by cross-dating. Prehistorians hopefully tried to bring the rest of the Continent into the time capsule. Amber was found in graves at Mycenae which had come from the shores of the Baltic Sea, so Greece must have had links with the north. Beads made from faience, a simple form of glass, appeared in the north, and it was thought that these originated in Greece. Megalithic tombs occurred in Spain, Brittany, the British Isles and Denmark, and Childe saw these as a manifestation of Aegean influence. About 2500 BC, he thought, traders from the east Mediterranean had arrived in Iberia in search of metal ores. With them they brought the tradition of communal burial in tombs made from large stones. From Spain their influence spread up the western seaboard after 2500 BC. Other traits could be seen: the spiral decoration on grave slabs above the shaft graves excavated by Schliemann at Mycenae was mirrored on the tomb of New Grange in Ireland. The development of copper-smelting in Spain, the defensive walls of the site of Los Millares and many other minor elements were assumed to reflect the eastern influence.

The second chain linking Europe and the Aegean ran, according to Childe, through the Balkans. Here again an elaborate and convincing system of cross-dating was built up on the assumption that the most important elements in the archaeology of northern Europe ultimately depended on the inspiration of the eastern Mediterranean and therefore must be later in date.

One of the areas most convincingly irradiated by Mycenaean influence was Britain. In addition to Megalithic tombs and faience beads Britain had Stonehenge. Its excavator, Richard Atkinson, wrote in 1960: 'Is it then any more incredible that the architect of Stonehenge should have been a Mycenaean, than that the monument should have been designed and erected, with all its unique and sophisticated detail, by mere barbarians?' Surrounding Stonehenge are many Bronze Age burial mounds, or at least there were before most of them succumbed to the tender mercies of modern cereal farmers. Some of these, such as Bush Barrow, have produced rich goldwork and

weapons, representative of what prehistorians call the Wessex Culture. Included among them were objects which were thought to show Mycenaean influence, reflecting the importance of Wessex as an intermediary in a supposed metal trade and by definition post-dating the Mycenaean originals of about 1500 BC.

So, on the basis of cross-dating ultimately derived from Egypt even distant Britain was slotted into the prehistoric network. The introduction of agriculture and the beginning of the Neolithic period were put just after 2000 BC and the start of the Bronze Age around 1500 BC.

In 1949 the American physicist Dr Willard F. Libby dropped a bombshell on the archaeological world. His discovery of radiocarbon dating, a revolutionary new method of dating the past, was a real time bomb, both literally and figuratively. There was also a delayed reaction before the full impact was felt by prehistorians.

Cosmic radiation of the earth's atmosphere results in the production of radioactive carbon. Normal carbon has an atomic weight of 12, while the radioactive isotope of carbon is slightly heavier with an atomic weight of 14, hence C-14. Radioactive carbon occurs in tiny quantities in comparison with Carbon-12, only one part in 0.8 billion (an English billion equals one million millions), and mixes evenly as carbon dioxide throughout the earth's atmosphere. During photosynthesis plants take up carbon dioxide, and as a result of eating plants so do animals. Consequently, all living things on earth contain equal proportions of radioactive carbon. Because C-14 is radioactive it decays at a constant rate: in fact, half of a given amount of radiocarbon will decay in about 5,700 years. In living creatures radiocarbon is absorbed at the same rate that it decays, and as a result the amount remains constant. Once the plant or animal dies, it no longer takes in C-14: that already in the body begins steadily to drain away like water leaking from a pail. As we know the original amount of radiocarbon in living organisms, it is possible to measure the proportion left in a sample and calculate the time since death. Wood, charcoal, seeds, animal bones and many other organic materials which are commonly found by archaeologists can be used for radiocarbon dating.

Of course, many problems have arisen with radiocarbon dating and these have been admirably described by Professor Renfrew and, more recently, by Dr Stuart Fleming.

The full impact of radiocarbon dating on the archaeological world depended on the development of dendrochronology, or tree-ring dating. In the White Mountains of California are found the world's oldest living inhabitants, the bristle-cone pines (*Pinus longaeva*), trees which reach the grand old age of 4,000 years. If a tree is cut down, we can see in its trunk a pattern of concentric rings. In these rings is fossilized the history of the tree, for each represents a year's growth. Dry years, disease, abundant rainfall—all leave their mark and result in a varying pattern of thin or thick rings. The dendrochronologist analyses this pattern and can equate each ring with a particular year. The

bristle-cone pine has a built-in calendar which, by the discovery of dead trees with overlapping sequences of rings, has been traced back about 8,200 years.

Many samples of wood which by dendrochronology could be dated absolutely were used to check the accuracy of radiocarbon dating. It was found that before 1200 BC radiocarbon dates were too young. In 1967 Dr Hans E. Suess, an American chemist and scientist, produced a graph which provided a means for calibrating radiocarbon dates. The reason for the discrepancies is probably that one of Libby's basic assumptions is incorrect: the proportion of Carbon-14 in the atmosphere has not remained constant. The dramatic consequence of Suess's graph was that sites dated to about 3000 BC had to be put back a further 800 years.

Colin Renfrew has described the effects of the 'Radiocarbon Revolution' in his book *Before Civilisation* (1973). Quite simply, radiocarbon dating has shattered the diffusionist image of prehistoric Europe. The elaborate network of interrelationships from the Mediterranean world across Europe can now be

Dendrochronology. Overlapping tree rings enable a precise calendar to be constructed from wood samples.

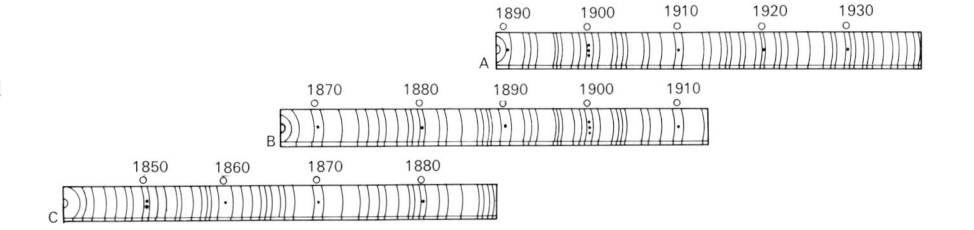

seen to have rested on a quaking foundation of false assumptions. The original links between Greece and Egypt still stand, and the accuracy of cross-dating has not been shaken. But north of Greece there is what Renfrew has vividly called an archaeological fault line. The cultural interrelationships within northern Europe hold good but they have all slipped down the time-scale as a result of radiocarbon dating. Megalithic tombs in Spain, France and Britain can no longer be derived from the Mediterranean. We can now see that they are themselves the oldest-known massive stone structures in the world. Similarly, the emergence of agriculture in northern Europe is put back to

Calibration curve covering the past 7,400 years produced as a result of the analysis of bristle-cone pine tree rings. The deviation of radiocarbon results becomes greater after about 1000 BC.

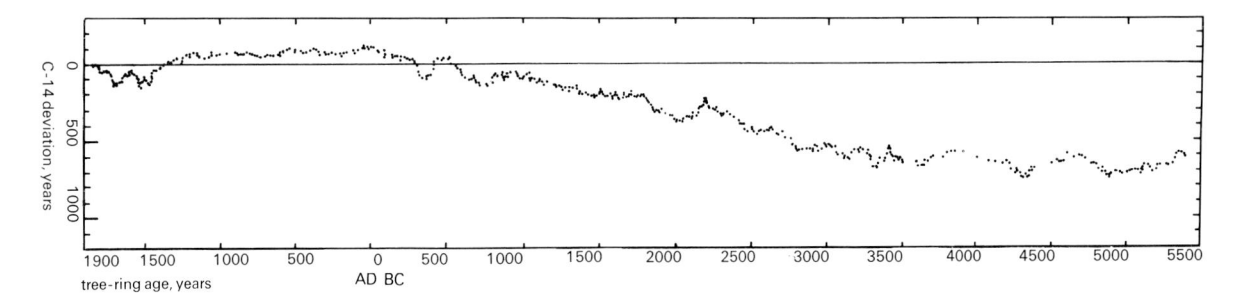

4000 BC, or earlier, and we no longer need to look for Mycenaean architects at Stonehenge (though some Mycenaean links may, arguably, still exist).

The collapse of the diffusionist view of European prehistory has created a different perspective among archaeologists. Radiocarbon dating enables us to compare world-wide developments, such as the origin of agriculture, in the Americas, Europe, Asia and the Far East, areas that previously could not be linked by cross-cultural chronologies. Archaeologists are gradually beginning to escape from the clichéd and blinkered diffusionist explanations and examine afresh the reasons for change in individual societies. The vigour and ingenuity of prehistoric communities can at last be appreciated without relying on 'the convenient arrival of wise men from the East'.

Radiocarbon dating is the most commonly used of the new dating techniques and has been the most dramatic in its effects. The archaeologist has, though, in recent years been the grateful, if somewhat confused, recipient of a whole battery of new dating methods developed by physicists. Thermoluminescence and Potassium-Argon dating are just two of these. The first is useful for dating fired clay, principally pottery, and can provide an alternative method to Carbon-14 dating where there is a lack of plant material or bone. One of the limitations of radiocarbon dating is that samples older than 60,000 years contain too little C-14 to be of any use. Potassium-Argon dating is a technique mainly used on rocks much older than this. It works on the familiar principle of measuring the decay of radioactive Potassium-40 isotopes. As Potassium-40 has a half-life of over 1,000 million years, samples themselves several thousand million years old can be dated. The Potassium-Argon method has been used on samples a mere 2,500 years old, but it is principally of use to archaeologists studying the fossils of early man.

3 Recognizing the past: archaeology in the countryside

Field-workers as far back as John Aubrey and William Stukeley have analysed the landscape in order to recognize and explain fossilized traces of man's past activities within it. In the 20s archaeologists like O. G. S. Crawford and Sir Cyril Fox extended our understanding of the man-made environment by their use of aerial photography and geographical techniques. More recently W. G. Hoskins with his book *The Making of the English Landscape* (1977) generated a wider awareness of the countryside as a living and complex historical document, not simply the result of eighteenth- and nineteenth-century Inclosure Acts, the handiwork of landscape gardeners or even just a factory floor for modern farmers. Hoskins awakened us to the possibility that a living hedge may be an estate boundary 1,000 years old, a lane may have been tramped by prehistoric traders, or a few humps and bumps in a field can represent the remains of an abandoned village.

One of the results of the 'Radiocarbon Revolution' has been to emphasize that an ancient community must be studied within its own region. Available resources such as land, water, building material, plants, animals, communications, the size of the human population, its social organization and beliefs all weave a complex but interrelated whole. The archaeologist who seeks to understand this must start with the evidence of the landscape itself.

It has often been said that the landscape of Britain is a palimpsest of human activity. Unfortunately this is true. 'Unfortunately' because a 'palimpsest' is a document which has been written on more than once, usually by erasing the original text. It is exactly the same with the face of the countryside: the labour of 300 generations has moulded what we see today, but much of that labour has been expended in destroying the evidence of our predecessors.

The survival of physical evidence of the past is dependent on many factors, and some areas are more favoured than others. The field archaeologist Christopher Taylor differentiates between what he calls 'the zone of survival and the zone of destruction'. To a large extent these coincide respectively with the moorland and pasture of the Highland zone in north and west Britain and the intensively farmed arable land of the south and east. In the survival zone archaeological features lie undisturbed beneath grassland instead of being destroyed by continual ploughing or other destructive forces.

Two hundred and fifty years ago the downlands of Wessex were among the

The formal landscape of Blenheim Park, Oxfordshire, with its avenue of elms originally laid out between 1710 and 1720 and replaced in 1901–2. Within the park much older earthworks are preserved. Running from centre bottom to top left is the line of the Roman Road, Akeman Street. The shadow to the right of Akeman Street, just beyond the avenue, indicates part of the earthworks of Grim's Ditch, a huge late Iron Age *oppidum*. Earthworks like these have long since been ploughed away in the arable fields which surround Blenheim Park.

Ingleborough, North Yorkshire: the highest and bleakest hill-fort in England at 723 m. The slight mounds of the Iron Age hut circles can still be seen here in the 'zone of survival'.

finest areas in Europe for viewing the handiwork of ancient man. William Stukeley proclaimed after striding over one of them: 'Tis a pretty round apex, the turf as soft as velvet. There is a sign of a very old camp cast up on one half of it but unfinished. The air here is extremely fragrant . . . the strolling for relaxed minds upon these downs is the most agreeable exercise and amusement in the world.' Abandoned settlements, burial mounds, the boundaries of ancient fields lay fossilized beneath Stukeley's beloved turf, emerging in low sunlight or a dusting of snow like a tracery of veins. These redundant works survived by chance because throughout the Middle Ages the downlands

were, mostly, extensive sheep pastures. Corn production became paramount with the Napoleonic Wars and again in recent years, and the vulnerable remains succumbed to the plough with the inevitability of sand-castles on the beach. The downs are now a zone of destruction, except for a few isolated islands of old pasture, in a sea of arable fields.

In much of upland Britain grazing is still the main form of land use, and preservation of sites is better. On land of little economic value such as moorland ancient sites are even more likely to be tolerated, though modern forestry schemes have recently done much damage. The zone of destruction is not without its interest, though. The gravel terraces of major river valleys like the Thames or the Trent have been cultivated continually for hundreds or even thousands of years. Successive generations of ploughmen have removed the visible evidence of their predecessors with monotonous regularity. Little of antiquity remains to be seen on these flat and featureless lands. Yet soon after World War I pioneer aviators like Major G. W. G. Allen produced a stream of photographs which startled the archaeological world. Flying solo, his joystick gripped between his knees, Allen recorded on film the evidence of 6,000 years of human occupation showing as crop marks in the ripening fields of barley 300 m below him.

Although there are no visible traces on the ground, the long roots of cereals can detect disturbance beneath them. Deposits of soil in ancient, silted ditches and pits provide a reservoir of nutrients and moisture which encourage plants over them to grow tall and dense. The effect is particularly spectacular on naturally free-draining subsoils such as gravel, because the moisture differential is especially high between damp buried features and the surrounding dry soil. Conversely, buried stone will stunt the crop and produce negative crop marks or parch marks. These effects can be seen in growing or ripening crops most often in June or July, and they mirror the buried remains with an uncanny accuracy.

Major G. W. G. Allen, one of the pioneers of archaeological aerial photography in Britain.

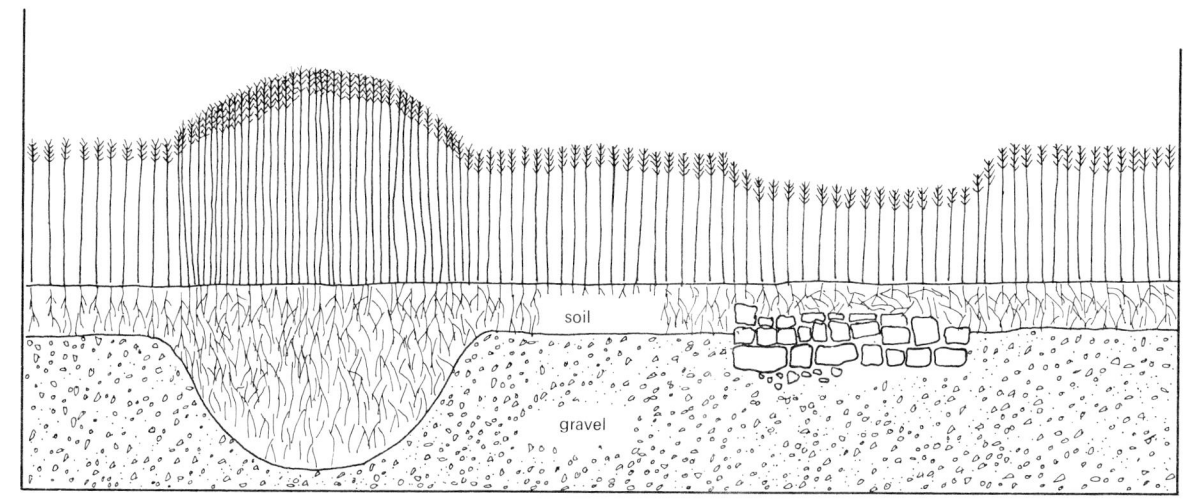

Above How crop marks develop. The cereals are taller over the buried ditch but stunted above the stone foundations.

Right A rare opportunity to see why crop marks appear. The dark soil of a silted-up Iron Age ditch appears in the face of this gravel pit. Above it the barley is distinctly taller as a result of the extra depth of soil and moisture.

In much of midland England grass covers the corrugated waves of medieval strip fields. This ridge and furrow is preserved but was itself responsible for the obliteration of earlier evidence. The unfavourable conditions for the recovery of prehistoric and Romano-British sites in the Midlands has encouraged some archaeologists to believe that the sites do not exist at all and that the heavy clay-lands were almost uninhabited. We must obviously beware of making generalizations from biased evidence.

The country-lover may regret the passing of familiar landscapes, but the archaeologist inevitably realizes that evolution and change are what he is attempting to study and understand. The evidence is complicated and fragmentary. Its analysis requires team-work on the part of historians, botanists, geologists, geomorphologists, zoologists and a forbidding battery of even more esoteric 'ologists'. Archaeologists themselves, bedevilled for the most part by the English segregation of arts and science subjects in school and university, have been reluctant to come to terms with the polymathic approach that the problems require. The trail was blazed by Grahame Clark in the 40s, but few had the inclination or resources to follow. Radiocarbon dating in some ways acted as a catalyst: besides bringing archaeologists hard up against

30

the world of physicists, it also enabled botanical and zoological samples to be dated accurately, forcing the not always reluctant archaeologists to consider new types of evidence.

The end of the last ice-age brought about a complete change in the British landscape and the way of life of the people who inhabited it. As the climate became warmer and glaciers melted, the sea-level rose drowning the shoreline habitation sites of Palaeolithic Man. The open tundra was colonized by thick forests, and the herds of reindeer and other cold-loving animals retreated northwards with the ice to be replaced by roe and red deer, elk and wild boar. There was less grazing available in the forests, the animals could not congregate in such large herds as the reindeer, and man had to adapt to his new environment.

In 1949 Johannes Iversen, a Danish geologist, wrote that 'primitive meso-lithic man was entirely dependent on nature; he could not interfere much with the vegetation'. That was the current view. The term 'Mesolithic', or Middle Stone Age, was applied to the communities which developed a 'hunting and gathering' way of life in the post-glacial period in response to their new environment. Recent research suggests that Iversen may have taken a rather pessimistic view of Mesolithic Man's ability to look after himself. There are indications that he was attempting to adapt his surroundings to make life easier for himself.

Our understanding of the Mesolithic way of life has changed drastically as a result of pollen analysis. Most plants disperse pollen into the air in order to propagate themselves. The pollen is made up of millions of microscopic grains which, when magnified, can be identified to a particular genus and, sometimes, species of plant. The pollen rains down on the surrounding countryside and in favourable circumstances, such as in peat bogs, is preserved almost indefinitely owing to its hard outer shell. By identifying and counting the pollen grains in a sample the palaeo-botanist can reconstruct the plant population of an area. Successive samples through a deep deposit of peat will reveal the changing pattern of vegetation through time.

In the warm post-glacial period from about 8000 BC tree pollen predominated —first birch and pine, then oak and hazel. But this fairly uniform landscape does not seem to have remained intact for very long. The image of the *forêt sauvage*, blanketing the country until medieval times, is a popular and romantic one and appears in many accounts of the British landscape, but 10,000 years ago our ancestors may have been making the first inroads.

There are no Mesolithic monuments in our landscape, but the people left their mark all the same. Ipping Common is a typical piece of Surrey heathland; it has been so since man cleared away the hazel woodland nearly 8,000 years ago. It is often assumed that only farmers need to remove the forests. There is now mounting evidence to suggest that the process was under way before agriculture, as we normally understand it, was taken up in Britain. At Star Carr in Yorkshire's Vale of Pickering Grahame Clark excavated a Mesolithic

occupation site. On the edge of a gravel mound by what was once a lake, the site had been buried by peat. In more recent times the marsh had been drained and turned into arable land, but beneath the peat waterlogged, airless conditions preserved the remains of the Mesolithic camp remarkably well. Yorkshiremen will be glad to know that when Star Carr was occupied their county stretched all the way to Denmark as the sea-level was still relatively low.

At Star Carr a platform of birch trunks and branches left no doubt that trees were being felled, even if on a small scale. Clark was able to show that the site had been occupied seasonally, through the winter until early spring, so that the hunters could remain close to the red deer which were their main food supply. Not only did this Mesolithic community follow the deer down into their sheltered winter feeding grounds but they also selectively culled the male deer and, 3,500 years before any other domestic animal had been discovered in this country, used dogs to help in the hunting.

The picture of human beings manipulating their environment is supported by a large number of pollen diagrams. At White Gill on the North Yorkshire Moors the first clearance of trees was made by hunting communities. Hunters in many parts of the world start forest fires in order to drive animals towards their traps; in addition they burn clearings, which encourages new and tender growth to spring up and attracts grazing animals. A slight increase in birch and hazel pollen at White Gill supports the idea of burning, as their deep roots make both of these trees resistant to fire.

The botanical remains, digging sticks, stone axes and animal bones show how Mesolithic people made an impact on their landscape, shaping their environment. The term Neolithic or New Stone Age is associated with the introduction of agriculture, the period of the first farmers and the domestication of animals. But we can be the victims of our own terms; they can create sharp divisions where none exist. The development of agriculture was not necessarily a great step for Mesolithic mankind. Many archaeologists assume that the 'Neolithic Revolution', like most other things, was introduced into Britain from outside. Where agriculture is concerned, diffusionism still prevails. To a certain extent this is justified as the wild progenitors of our cereals undeniably originated in the Near East; however, the processes of plant and animal manipulation which characterize farming were under way before the beginning of the Neolithic period in the fourth millennium BC. The indigenous population was ready to take advantage of the remarkable new plants and animals and the opportunities they offered for a fully-fledged farming economy.

The introduction of farming in the fourth millennium BC and our reliance on it ever since has been the single biggest factor in the appearance of the British landscape. But farming and rural settlement have not remained static; the growth of population, developing technology, new ideas and many other factors have resulted in changing patterns of land use and the appearance of new monuments.

It is unfortunate but inevitable that the soils most suitable for agriculture have been continually dug or ploughed for thousands of years. Very little physical evidence of Neolithic farming survives, yet it is of paramount importance if we are to understand how and why agriculture developed. Stone axes and hoes from Neolithic sites show that the land was being cleared; quern-stones suggest that corn was ground; and traces of the actual grains are sometimes found impressed into what is the earliest pottery in the British Isles. Grain can also survive if it has been carbonized by being close to a fire. We know that Neolithic farmers grew at least three types of wheat, emmer and einkorn and bread wheat, and also barley. In addition they kept cattle, sheep and pigs. Remarkable evidence for the earliest use of a plough occurred under the Neolithic South Street long barrow near Avebury in Wiltshire. A criss-cross pattern of lines cut into the old ground surface underneath the burial mound indicated that before the barrow was built the land had been cultivated. Strictly speaking these marks were caused not by a plough, which turns the soil over, but by an ard, a primitive scratch plough. The fact that the lines criss-crossed one another showed that the field had been ploughed in two directions so that the soil would be completely broken up by the far from powerful ard. The plough marks, incidentally, suggest that Neolithic farmers had already learnt to castrate cattle in order to use them as draught animals. This method of cultivation usually results in small, squarish fields.

Yorkshire Dales: field patterns under snow. Beneath the modern pasture bounded by stone walls can be seen the characteristic earthworks of small, rectangular prehistoric and Romano-British fields, medieval strip lynchets and post-medieval narrow rig cultivation.

North Marefield, Leicestershire. The streets, lanes, tofts and crofts of this deserted medieval village can be seen under the modern pasture. Among the village earthworks the sun gleams on the water in the moat around the site of the manor-house. Deep shadows throw into relief the corrugated sea of strip fields surrounding the village. At the top left-hand corner of the picture modern ploughing has removed all traces of the medieval landscape.

In the medieval period a heavy mould-board plough was drawn by a team of six or eight oxen. This plough turned the soil efficiently, but the large team made turning round difficult. This was one factor in the development in medieval times of the narrow strip field, which enabled the ploughmen to keep going in one direction as long as possible. In contrast the Neolithic farmer with his ard, scratching the soil in two directions, would find a squarish field more advantageous. Fields of this shape, misleadingly called Celtic fields, continued in use into the Roman period. Where they survive on hill slopes or on the top of downland as a chequer-board of shallow banks, they usually represent the high-water mark of arable activity. The prevalence of Celtic fields on chalk downland has encouraged the view that prehistoric man preferred to cultivate and live on the light chalk soils, while the lowland remained wooded. This is probably wrong; for most lowland soils have been ploughed continually, which has destroyed the early remains there and left only the upland fields undisturbed.

Preservation of the ancient landscape is best in the rocky areas of the west. In Cornwall or, to take the most extreme case, the Aran Islands of western Ireland vast quantities of stones had to be cleared off the land to make agriculture possible. These are usually piled up as thick walls or cairns and serve to protect the crops from strong winds. This creates built-in conservatism. Changing the field pattern becomes a colossal task, and as a result the fields in use today often date back to prehistoric times though even here modern bulldozers are beginning to have drastic effects.

The shape of fields is determined then by the underlying geology, the technological level of the farmer and the use to which they are to be put, for example, as stock pens or for growing crops. These factors can often influence the appearance of the landscape over long periods, and economic common sense may lead to the retention of a particular pattern of land use. Studies at Grime's Graves in the Breckland of Norfolk show that the modern system of livestock, barley and legume production is similar to that practised about 4,000 years ago in the same area. Recent attempts to change it have led to soil erosion by wind blows.

Conservatism is a strong factor in developed agricultural economies, but the study of pollen illustrates the changes that Neolithic people brought about. At Ballyscullion in Ireland's Bann Valley three phases can be recognized: firstly, small-scale forest clearance, represented by a small decline in the amount of elm pollen and an increase in grasses, then a period of farming, marked by an increase in weed species such as ribwort plantain (*Plantago lanceolata*). In fact, not only botanists recognize this plant as an agricultural indicator. During the early European colonization of Eastern America the Indians called plantain 'Englishman's foot', as it appeared wherever he trod. The first clearings at Ballyscullion were then abandoned, and forest regenerated only to be cleared on a larger scale. The third phase of extensive clearance is sometimes known as the 'elm decline'. It used to be thought that climatic change brought this about, but it is now generally accepted that man was to blame.

The general picture is of a gradually expanding agricultural economy and an increasing human population. Unfortunately, the actual occupation sites of early prehistoric farmers are notoriously difficult to find in Britain. In contrast their burial mounds are very much in evidence. In the early sixteenth century Sir John Oglander of Nunwell, Isle of Wight, said 'you may see divers buries on ye toppe of our Island Hills', while John Leland observed on Salisbury Plain 'sepultures of men of warre . . . in divers places of the playne'. These long and round barrows surviving on the unploughed uplands of southern England greatly attracted the necrophiliac antiquaries of the nineteenth century. Their hearty approach is conveyed in the Reverend Isaacson's poem 'Barrow Digging by a Barrow Knight' (1845):

> *Uprouse ye then, my barrow digging men,*
> *It is our opening day!*
> *And all exclaimed, their grog whilst swigging,*
> *There's naught on earth like barrow digging!*

The preservation of burial mounds and other earthworks on the downs, at least until recently, has attracted archaeologists and led to an undue emphasis on chalk upland at the expense of lowland areas. Barrows are a familiar sight in Cornwall, Devon, Wessex, the Cotswolds and the Peak District, though rapidly disappearing as intensive arable agriculture encroaches on them.

Long barrows, the burial mounds of our Neolithic ancestors, are the earliest man-made structures that survive in southern Britain. Approximately 330 of them are known, some constructed of earth mounded over timber structures and others with stone chambers. The earthen long barrow at Lambourn in Berkshire has provided the earliest radiocarbon date of 3,415 ± 180, which when calibrated gives a date of approximately 4340 BC. Somewhat later is the long barrow of Giant Hills in Lincolnshire with calibrated dates about 3000 BC. This form of burial mound was probably in use for about 1,000 years. By calculating the total number of burials (the average is ten to fifteen per barrow with a maximum of fifty-seven) Professor Atkinson estimated that the population of southern England about 3000 BC was between 70 and 140 people. This is obviously a considerable underestimate of the likely total, but what it does suggest is that long barrows were not communal burial places for egalitarian agricultural communities. It appears that only a small proportion of people were buried in them; the rest, possibly of lower status, must have been disposed of in ways which left no archaeological trace.

This illustrates the approach archaeologists are now adopting: burial mounds and cemeteries in general are not seen simply as a potential quarry for pretty objects. They can tell us about burial practices, the health and age structure of part of the population; they cover buried soils which contain valuable biological evidence; and their distribution can give an indication of the size of the territories occupied by their builders. This last point has been clearly illustrated by Colin Renfrew on the Orkney Island of Rousay. There the

Midhowe chambered cairn, Rousay, Orkney. The monument is roofed over in order to protect it from the weather.

36

Neolithic funeral mounds are known to archaeologists as chambered tombs because they have been skilfully built as drystone burial chambers encased within an earthen mound. Rousay is in Christopher Taylor's 'zone of preservation', and less intensive agriculture results in thirteen surviving tombs, possibly the total number that existed. The other great advantage of Rousay as a study area is that it is an island. This means that its boundaries are obvious, by no means a simple problem when considering prehistoric territories in southern England. As one wit remarked: 'The number of different boundaries for any region is equal to the square of the number of geographers consulted.' All thirteen of Rousay's chambered tombs are situated near its narrow strip of arable land. Taking this geographical distribution, Renfrew has suggested that each one represents an individual farming community cultivating a share of the decent land and that 'for each community, the monument was not just the ancestral tomb but an enduring symbol of its occupation of the land'. The maximum population for each of these territories could be about fifty people but it was probably considerably less. Once we have some idea of population numbers, then we can begin, seriously, to discuss the social structure.

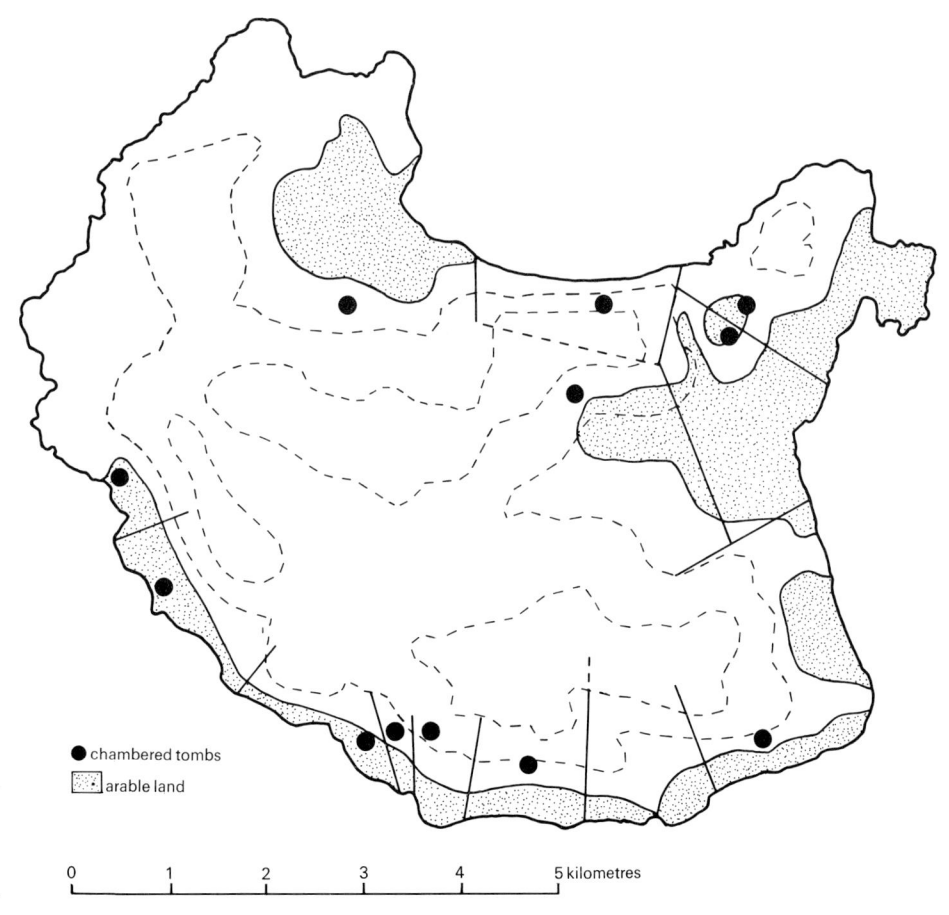

● chambered tombs

▨ arable land

| 0 | 1 | 2 | 3 | 4 | 5 kilometres |

Rousay, Orkney: the relationship of chambered tombs and modern arable land (stippled). An island with good preservation of sites presents the archaeologist with the opportunity to study hypothetical territories.

37

Obviously, though, at each stage of such an argument the archaeologist is treading further and further out on to the quaking bog of speculation.

By about 2000 BC burial habits had changed, at least for that section of society whose graves are still visible in the form of round barrows. Unlike long barrows, the round ones of the Bronze Age, often associated with the so-called Beaker folk, can contain a single burial, occasionally with quite rich grave goods, like the gold earrings at Radley, Oxfordshire, or the gold-studded dagger, gold mounts and stone sceptre in Bush Barrow near Stonehenge. Bronze Age barrows come in all shapes and sizes, and it would be an over-simplification to imagine they all contain a single inhumation. Some have more than one burial, and often cremation is practised. There is also considerable regional variation. In southern England barrows can occur in large numbers. In the Ridgeway area of Dorset there are at least 438, that is, ten per square mile, and around Stonehenge they are even thicker on the ground with twenty-five per square mile. The density of barrows is also high in the river valleys, but nowadays they usually appear only as circular marks in growing cereals, their mounds long since flattened by ploughing. By 2000 BC evidently much of the countryside was open, for many of the barrows are sited so as to be visible from a distance.

In spite of the fact that Neolithic and Bronze Age burial mounds are relatively common, contemporary settlements tend to elude the archaeologist. This may be because prehistoric farmers were nomadic, or at least shifted around as the soil became exhausted, and their houses were slight. On the whole this seems unlikely, and certainly on the Continent large Neolithic communities built large and impressive long houses, the foundations of which are preserved under deep deposits of wind-blown loess soils. On the chalklands conditions are not favourable for the discovery of the post-holes of timber buildings constructed as much as 6,000 years ago. Slightly acidic rain-water dissolves and lowers the surface of the chalk at the rate of about 8 cm per 1,000 years, and this could account for the disappearance of shallow foundations. In other areas erosion on the higher ground, caused by agriculture, created an accumulation of soil in the valley bottoms which may have buried early settlements. If this is so, then the settlements have yet to turn up.

It seems likely that with increasingly large-scale and careful excavation Neolithic occupation sites will be discovered. One classic site has been known since 1850 when a storm shifted the sand-dunes at Skara Brae in Orkney and uncovered a stone-built Neolithic village in a remarkable state of preservation. The walls of the houses there stand up to 3 m high, and the square rooms are 4.5–6 m across. Inside are beds and cupboards made of slabs of Caithness flagstone and central hearths also edged with stone. The roofs may have been of sod supported by whalebones but have long since collapsed.

Elsewhere in Britain settlements are less substantial, but recent excavations are beginning to bring them to light. At Fengate, near Peterborough, work on a massive scale paid off in 1972 with the discovery of the foundations of a

Skara Brae, Orkney: the inside of a Neolithic house, preserved by blown sand, with its hearth, bed bases, storage boxes and stone 'welsh-dresser'.

Abbot's Way, Somerset. This corduroy timber trackway, dating to about 2000 BC, is preserved beneath the peat of the Somerset Levels. It is one of a network of tracks running across the marshy ground, linking prehistoric settlements on the nearby higher ground and dry islands within the marsh.

rectangular hut 7 m by 8.5 m. Pottery of the type found associated with this building has been dated to the fourth millennium BC. In the marshes of the Somerset Levels Neolithic and Bronze Age timber trackways are continually revealed as peat is extracted for the nation's flowerpots. Their study is revealing a complex communications' network which links the surrounding hills and dry sandy islands within the Levels. Presumably it is on these islands that settlements must be sought; unfortunately, they are still covered by villages.

There are other substantial monuments of this period that have been known to archaeologists for a long time but have been interpreted by the catch-all phrase 'ritual sites'. Causewayed camps or, to give them their more recent if more cumbersome title, 'interrupted-ditch enclosures' are now known as a result of aerial photography to occur throughout southern England. They usually consist of one to four concentric rings of ditches with irregularly spaced but frequent entrances or causeways through them, enclosing up to 8 hectares at Windmill Hill in Wiltshire. In spite of a number of excavations, the light that has been shed on their function is distinctly dim. It is customary to see them as tribal or regional centres or, in the current jargon, 'central places' where groups of Neolithic people would come together at certain times of year to trade, hold religious festivals and find marriage partners. In other words they probably functioned very much like the medieval fair with its mixture of secular and religious activities. Prehistorians usually claim that causewayed camps were not occupied all year round, but there seems little justification for saying this.

The traditional picture of the Neolithic is of peaceable agriculturalists and herdsmen free of the economic pressures which result in warfare. Recent excavations at the causewayed camp of Crickley Hill in Gloucestershire and Carn Brae, Devon, have produced evidence of burning and large numbers of

The Neolithic henge monument of Avebury, Wiltshire, with its massive external bank still surviving. Silbury Hill is in the background.

arrowheads, which suggests we should modify our view. It is well known that tribesmen in New Guinea have indulged in habitual conflict in spite of or because of their Neolithic cultural level.

In the later Neolithic and early Bronze Age we no longer find causewayed camps; instead, the most dominant man-made structures in the landscape are earthwork enclosures, usually called henge monuments. The name comes from the 'hanging stones' of Stonehenge, a feature unfortunately not associated with the rest of these enclosures. Henge monuments come in a variety of sizes, but what characterizes them is a circular bank with an internal ditch. Where suitable stone occurs nearby, at Avebury, for example, or the Ring of Brogar in Orkney, then stone circles may be constructed inside the enclosure. In recent years Geoffrey Wainwright has carried out an extensive campaign of excavation on some of Wessex's largest henges at Marden and Durrington Walls in Wiltshire and Mount Pleasant near Dorchester, Dorset. Inside these Wainwright located massive circular timber buildings. The largest one, at Durrington Walls, was about 39 m in diameter with a roof supported on five concentric rings of posts.

One of the most interesting exercises that has been carried out in recent British prehistoric studies is to estimate the human resources necessary to construct the various types of tribal centre. The largest of the causewayed camps, Windmill Hill, would have taken Neolithic men armed with antler picks and baskets about 120,000 man-hours to construct. Five centuries later one and a half million man-hours were expended on the Avebury henge. Geoffrey Wainwright has underlined the effort that was required with his estimation that the large Durrington house consumed 264 tonnes of oak timber, and that represents almost 4 hectares of oak forest. Throughout the Neolithic period in Britain the human population seems to have expanded, societies (tribes, perhaps) were dominating greater areas, and their central places were becoming progressively larger.

On the gravel terraces of the Thames Valley centuries of arable farming have infilled even the huge ditches of the Big Rings henge monument near Dorchester, Oxfordshire. This site was only discovered by aerial photography when crop marks appeared over its buried ditches.

Professor Thom's suggestion that stone circles and some henges had an astronomical significance is, to varying degrees, now accepted by many archaeologists. Certainly, these earthworks are generally assumed to have had a ceremonial function. Wainwright, however, has emphasized that seasonal tribal gatherings inextricably combined the religious and the secular in a way that modern man is inclined to forget. What these monuments certainly do show is that Neolithic and Bronze Age communities steadily developed, became more settled and were able to muster growing numbers to work on the principal 'public' monuments.

It has already been pointed out that archaeologists can easily become the victims of their own terms. If 'henges' conjure up the automatic response 'religion', then the very name 'hill-fort' leads us to think in terms of warfare and defence. To a certain extent this may be justified: the great ramparts which dominate the skyline in so many parts of Britain were obviously constructed with security in mind; but to see them just as forts is an over-simplification.

In the later Bronze Age we have evidence for the extensive and well-organized cultivation of the land in the form of huge blocks of fields laid out systematically. The introduction of ironworking must have speeded up the clearance of the forest in two ways: firstly, iron tools, widely available and cheap, can do the job more efficiently; and, secondly, the production of iron itself requires large quantities of charcoal, which could only be obtained by making inroads into the remaining woodland.

Whereas earlier prehistoric occupation sites are difficult to locate, from the beginning of the Iron Age settlements of all types are common—simple farms, villages, temporary seasonal sites, hill-forts and, later, the large *oppida* of the period just before the Roman Conquest in AD 43. The obviously expanding population was probably supplemented by immigrants from the Continent. Although 'invasion hypotheses' have gone out of fashion, someone had to introduce the Celtic language. A lot of effort has gone into the excavation of

Dun Aengus, Inishmore, Aran Islands. The builders of this impressive clifftop fort made use of the limestone that lay all around them. Protected on one side by the huge Atlantic breakers, the landward approach was defended by a bristling belt of jagged spikes of rock, a *chevaux de frise*, the answer to the Celtic chariot. On this massive limestone slab of an island there is little need to rob stone from existing buildings, and prehistoric monuments such as this remain remarkably intact.

Iron Age farmsteads and villages in order to understand their structure and economy, but some of the most interesting recent work has been on the dominant hill-forts.

Radiocarbon dating has shown surprisingly early origins for some hill-forts calibrated to 1470 BC at Mam Tor in Derbyshire and 1100 BC at Dinorben in Denbighshire. One effect of this is to make us realize that our time divisions, such as Bronze Age and Iron Age, are arbitrary ones invented by archaeologists: they encourage us to parcel up the past into stereotyped, neat, but potentially artificial packages. The stage was not cleared for the benefit of historians: just as many elements of the Neolithic continue into the Bronze Age, so the latter now seems to blend into the Iron Age. The hill-forts should, perhaps, be seen as successors of the causewayed camps and henges in the British landscape—tribal centres fulfilling a number of roles. The discovery of shrines or temples inside hill-forts, such as South Cadbury, Somerset, Maiden Castle, Dorset, and Danebury, Hampshire, confirms the importance of religion; large storage pits for agricultural produce, granaries and imported goods emphasize their role in the storage and distribution of goods; the massive banks and ditches of Maiden Castle or the entrances of Danebury, elaborately constructed for the benefit of guards armed with sling-shots, vividly convey the need for defence. Elsewhere in Britain Celtic defences take a rather different form with the startling stone towers and brochs of northern Scotland or the stone forts of western Ireland, particularly Dun Aengus in the Aran Islands which resembles a fossilized porcupine with its encircling forest of jagged limestone spikes, a *chevaux de frise*, the ultimate in anti-chariot warfare.

The military role of hill-forts should not be over-emphasized. While some enclosures contain little evidence of internal occupation and may have been used as corrals for animals, others are packed with houses, sometimes showing elements of internal planning. When Suetonius described the Roman invasion, he called them *oppida*, or towns, and it is in this light that we should consider them.

42

4 Recognizing the past: archaeology in towns

The British are the most urbanized people in the world; only 3.5 per cent of us live and work on the land. It has not always been so. About 1600 Girolamo Lando, a Venetian, recorded that England 'does not possess many large towns, a small number for its size, but has very frequent and populous villages and small towns'. By 1771, however, Matthew Bramble, the irascible and forthright hero of Smollett's *Humphry Clinker*, could bemoan the spread of the metropolis: 'London is literally new to me; new in its streets, houses and even in its situation; as the Irishman said "London is now gone out of town". What I left open fields, producing hay and corn, I now find covered with streets and squares, and palaces, and churches. I am credibly informed, that in the space of seven years eleven thousand new houses have been built in one quarter of Westminster, exclusive of what is daily added to other parts of this unwieldy metropolis. Pimlico and Knightsbridge are now almost joined to Chelsea and Kensington, and if this infatuation continues for half a century, I suppose the whole county of Middlesex will be covered in brick . . . the capital is become an overgrown monster; which, like a dropsical head, will in time leave the body and extremities without nourishment and support.'

As a nation of town- or suburb-dwellers we remain romantically attached to the idyll of the countryside. The eighteenth-century gentleman with his country house and the frustrated bank-holiday tourist caught in a Lake District traffic jam are a reflection of the British antipathy towards undiluted town-dwelling, or as Keats wrote:

> To one who has been long in city pent
> 'Tis very sweet to look into the fair
> And open face of heaven.

Perhaps the traditional lack of commitment to town-dwelling, combined with familiarity, has led to a certain indifference towards the urban environment. Certainly, the treatment meted out to our towns in the 50s and 60s by some planners and developers could only be paralleled in its insensitivity by that of the *Luftwaffe* a couple of decades earlier.

If the urban redevelopment of the 60s resulted in the irrevocable loss of much that was admirable (and much that was not) in our towns, at least it jolted archaeologists awake. On the Continent the improbable launching pads

of urban archaeology were the scars left by World War II air raids—the bomb-sites. German archaeologists seized the opportunity offered by these devastated areas, in cities like Cologne, to excavate the rich layers previously inaccessible beneath buildings. In England, with a few notable exceptions— for example, at Exeter—there was little interest in urban archaeology after the war. By the 60s the historic cores of our towns were being gutted on such a scale that it was belatedly realized that we were in danger of losing not only many of our oldest buildings but the archaeological deposits which lay beneath them. In towns like London, Canterbury and Cambridge the material evidence of their origin, growth and development was daily bulldozed away. But like all redevelopment programmes, clearance within urban areas creates opportunities, and the last fifteen years have seen a surge of interest in the study of our towns. Increasingly, excavation is showing that many towns are much older than was previously suspected, but the origins of urbanism in Britain do not always have to be sought beneath concrete and tarmac. Towns, like any other organism, can develop and flourish or wither and die. Excavation is obviously much easier on a deserted site, uncluttered by buildings and roads, but while failed towns are of great interest, the urban archaeologist must try to get to the roots of living communities.

Until recently it was believed that our urban roots were transplanted by the Roman conquerors of Britain in the first century after Christ. Tacitus informs us that his father-in-law Agricola 'gave private encouragement and official assistance to the building of temples, public squares and private mansions'. In other words he tried to make the Britons civilized, in the original sense of that word, by encouraging the construction of the major elements of the Roman town—the religious centre, the market and seat of government and also the private investment in town houses.

Agricola was not sowing the seeds of urbanism on stony ground. The Celtic tribesmen of southern Britain were settled agriculturalists, who were involved in extensive trading and even minted their own coinage. As we have already heard, Suetonius called their major settlements *oppida*, or towns, and we know from aerial photography and excavation that some hill-forts were densely occupied. Can we really think of these places as towns? What, in fact, is a town? One possible definition is a place where there is a *relatively* dense, permanent concentration of people, of different classes, involved to varying degrees in administration, trade and industry.

Until recently excavation at British hill-forts usually consisted of a section cut through the ramparts and possibly a few key-hole trenches in the interior. As a result there was a tendency to see the hill-fort as a set of defensive banks around an empty space—a place of temporary refuge rather than a permanent and densely occupied settlement. Area excavation and aerial photography have rectified this picture. Not only were the interiors often crowded, but the sites themselves occupy a position at the end of a chain of settlement. Surrounding them in the countryside are dependent hamlets, farms and fields.

At South Cadbury in Somerset evidence of dense occupation was found during excavations by Leslie Alcock between 1967 and 1970. Substantial round houses, pits for underground storage of corn and other produce and large deposits of rubbish indicate that the settlement was not temporary or seasonal. High-class craftsmen making armour and bronze objects worked in South Cadbury alongside the more lowly potters, weavers and blacksmiths. A flat bar of iron, pinched at one end, was discovered. Caesar says that the Britons used iron rods of specific weights as a form of money, and for this reason objects of this kind are known as currency bars. These bars may indicate some form of commerce at South Cadbury, and certainly trading was going on as imported pottery was found there.

Leslie Alcock also discovered a small rectangular structure, which was detectable where six posts penetrated the ground. Around it was a group of pits in which the skulls of horses and cattle had been carefully placed. It is something of a cliché that when an archaeologist cannot explain his evidence he claims that it is a ritual site. In spite of this, Alcock's interpretation of this building as a shrine is credible. At the very end of the Celtic occupation the hill-fort was attacked; men, women and children were massacred; and the defences breached. Inside the gateway a large number of brooches and other evidence indicated that there had been, in the excavator's words, 'traders' booths and stalls . . . to catch the attention of rustics and their wives as they brought their goods to market'. These had been thrown down and destroyed in the attack on Cadbury.

At South Cadbury we seem to have most of the elements of an early town: permanent buildings, a religious centre, craftsmen servicing customers of varying rank, storage of produce, trade with the outside world and shops. A similar picture is emerging at several other hill-forts, notably at Danebury in Hampshire, where Barry Cunliffe has found streets and another possible shrine among the clusters of storage pits. Here, round houses have been found only where the foundations were protected under earth washed down from the inside of the hill-fort ramparts. Elsewhere on the site their existence is suspected, but nothing remains for the excavator.

In excavations between 1960 and 1966 at Croft Ambrey in Herefordshire S. C. Stanford also found evidence of intensive occupation inside the hill-fort. Many Iron Age houses are circular, but at Croft Ambrey there are groups of post-holes forming squares, with sides 3–4 m long. These are regularly laid out, and although less than 4 per cent of the interior of the hill-fort was excavated, it has been suggested that the whole of the site was covered with rows of these rectangular structures. A similar arrangement can be seen at Crickley Hill, Gloucestershire, where lines of post-holes have been interpreted as long, rectangular buildings alongside a roadway. An alternative theory is that these post-holes are the foundations of above-ground storage units and not houses at all.

Not only excavation but aerial photography can reveal the character of

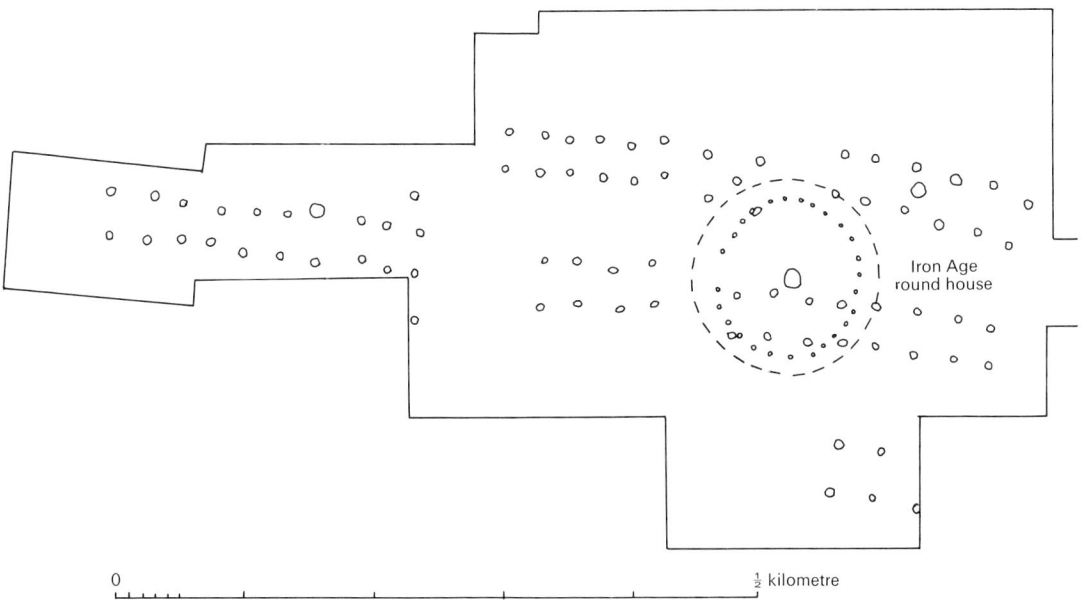

Iron Age
round house

0   ½ kilometre

Above Crickley Hill,
Gloucestershire.

Right Crickley Hill,
Gloucestershire. The
area excavation inside
this Iron Age hill-fort
has uncovered a large
circular house and
several straight lines of
post-holes. The latter
are the subject of much
debate. Some
archaeologists believe
they indicate
rectangular long-houses,
rarely identified in
Celtic Britain but
common on the
Continent, and others
that they belong to
timber granaries with
four to six posts each
sitting side by side.

46

hill-fort interiors. At Dyke Hills, Dorchester, Oxfordshire, crop marks show the outlines of dozens of hut circles and storage pits covering 45 hectares in a loop of the Thames and defended by a massive bank and ditch. As the ground here is flat and low-lying, we can hardly call Dyke Hills a hill-fort. It is closer to the class of late Iron Age defended areas, known, perhaps confusingly, as *oppida*. When Suetonius used the word, he was referring to hill-forts; as a modern archaeological term it means the latest type of major Celtic settlement appearing in the late first century BC or early years of the Christian era. *Oppida* are found in southern England often on fairly low ground and are not confined to hilltops. The banks which defend them are normally discontinuous, perhaps originally linking areas of woodland or marsh in order to control access to the interior which may be quite extensive. The *oppidum* at Colchester incorporates as much as 3,108 hectares.

Dyke Hills, Dorchester, Oxfordshire: part of the densely occupied internal area of this large (45-hectare) late Iron Age settlement. Hut circles, ditched enclosures and storage pits are revealed as crop marks in the growing barley.

Little excavation has been done inside *oppida*, but at Bagendon, an 81-hectare *oppidum* in Gloucester and tribal centre of the Dobunni, there was evidence for a mint producing coins. The *oppidum* is probably the most sophisticated form of settlement in Britain on the eve of the Roman Conquest.

We must not forget that other parts of Britain were more conservative and less open to Continental influences. Hill-forts were in use for about 1,000 years, and their functions varied and evolved. They cannot automatically be associated with urbanization; each must be assessed in its own right. In the Pennines traces of hut circles can still be seen inside the highest hill-fort in the country, Ingleborough, but there is no evidence that this bleak and inhospitable site was in any way urbanized.

With the coming of the Romans, towns take on a more familiar appearance, but it is now apparent that Mediterranean civilization was not imposed on a totally reluctant and rural British population. The process of urbanization had been under way for a long time. This continuity and evolution of tribal or regional centres can best be seen at the two Dorchesters of Oxfordshire and Dorset. We can see that Dorchester, Oxfordshire, acted as a regional centre for over 2,000 years. First, there was a major Neolithic complex with a large

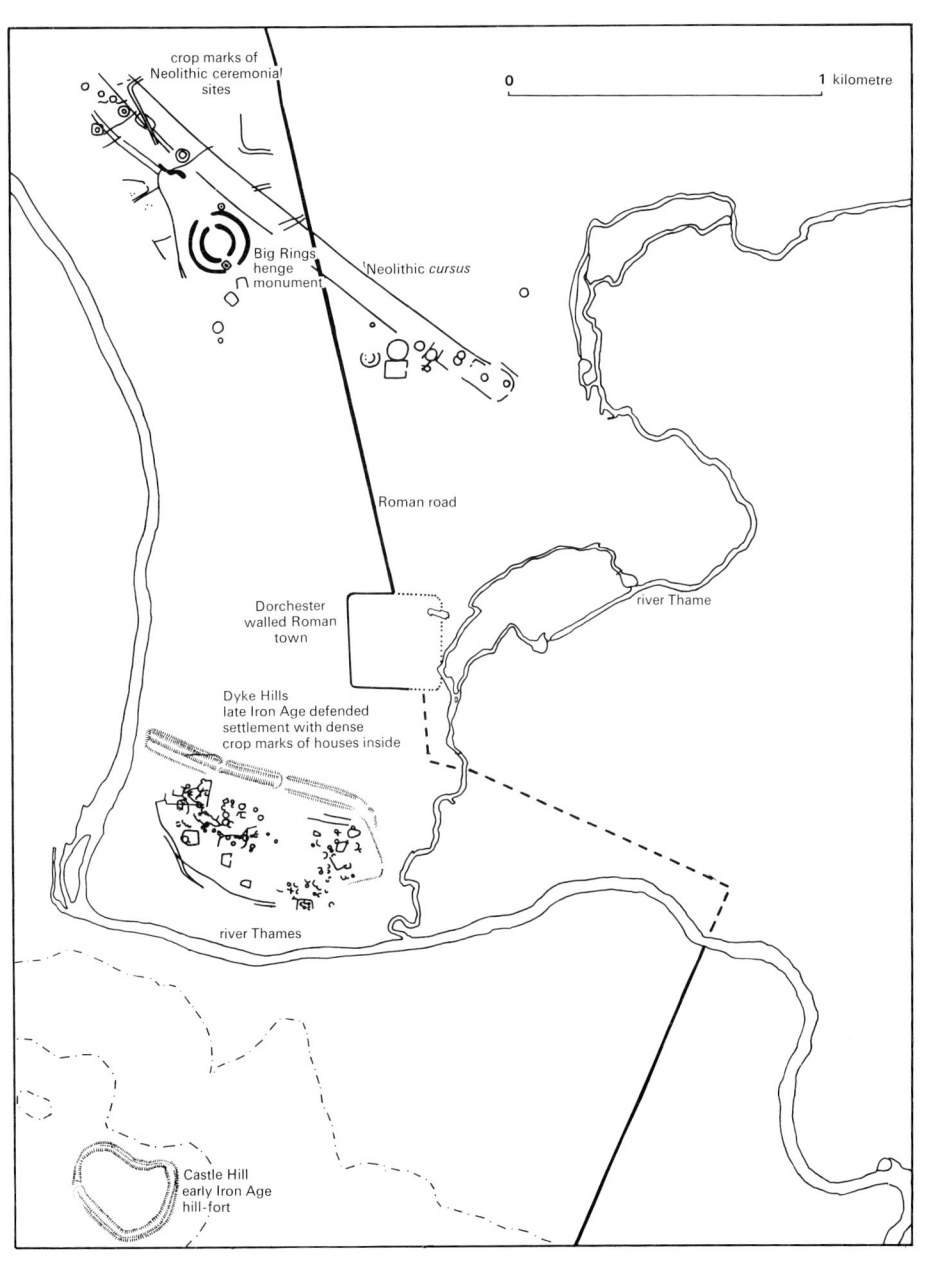

Dorchester, Oxfordshire: a regional centre from Neolithic times until the late Saxon period.

earthwork enclosure, *cursus* and small henges. In the early Iron Age a hill-fort dominated the Thames from the chalk eminence of Sinodun. By the time of the Conquest Dyke Hills, near the river, was the nucleus of settlement; Sinodun had been abandoned. In the early years after the Conquest a Roman military fort stood just outside Dyke Hills, no doubt keeping an eye on the locals. The soldiers were probably not needed for very long, and by the end of the first century AD a small Romanized town stood at Dorchester, linked by road to Silchester in the south and Alchester to the north. But this Roman town was not planted in a vacuum. In the first century AD it was the latest in a long line of social, trading, religious and military centres on this site at the confluence of Thames and the Thame.

Dorchester, Dorset, has a similar development. About 3000 BC a causewayed camp occupied the site known as Maiden Castle. A thousand years later the main focus was on the opposite side of a shallow valley at Mount Pleasant, with its large henge or earthwork enclosure. This was succeeded about 1700 BC by a settlement on the hilltop of 4.5 hectares, enclosed within a strong palisade. In the first millennium BC Maiden Castle was again occupied, and construction started on the complicated series of hill-fort ramparts, culminating in the massive defences which faced the Romans. The prehistoric fondness for hilltops was ignored by the Romans, who built the new town of Durnovaria on the present lower site of Dorchester by the river crossing.

The deliberate policy of abandoning native sites, probably breaching their defences and creating a planned Roman town nearby, can be seen at many other places. We have already mentioned the *oppidum* of Bagendon. Its replacement proved to be one of the most successful of Roman towns—Cirencester.

Most major Romano-British towns began life as military camps. The sites were chosen by military commanders with strategic aims uppermost in their minds, sometimes, but not always, near to a native settlement. The skill of these men is attested by the fact that the majority of their foundations are occupied to the present day. A few Roman towns like Silchester were later abandoned and today lie beneath fields whose pattern may reflect the outline of the town. The fact that Silchester is unencumbered by modern buildings is a great advantage to archaeologists, and for this reason the site has been extensively excavated. Work was carried out principally between 1890 and 1909, unfortunately not very well by today's standards. The excavations showed that the Roman town was preceded by a Celtic settlement, which about AD 5 was the tribal capital of the northern Atrebates under their leader Eppillus. He had coins minted which included his own name and that of the town, Calleva. Aerial photographs show the polygonal outline of the Roman town—part of its walls still stand—and the regular grid of streets inside. The streets divided the town into blocks or *insulae* upon which stood houses and shops, and at the centre lay the forum, the commercial and administrative heart of every major Roman town. The central piazza of the forum was 43 m by 40 m with a covered arcade around the north, south and east side behind

Right Silchester, Berkshire: the tribal capital of the Atrebates. The polygonal outline of the Romano-British town is preserved in the modern field pattern. The street pattern shows as a grid of light-coloured lines where the modern crops are parched and stunted over the buried stone. The straight hedge at the top of the picture is the line of the Roman Road to London.

Below Allen Farrell's reconstruction of Silchester, Berkshire, looking west.

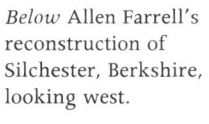

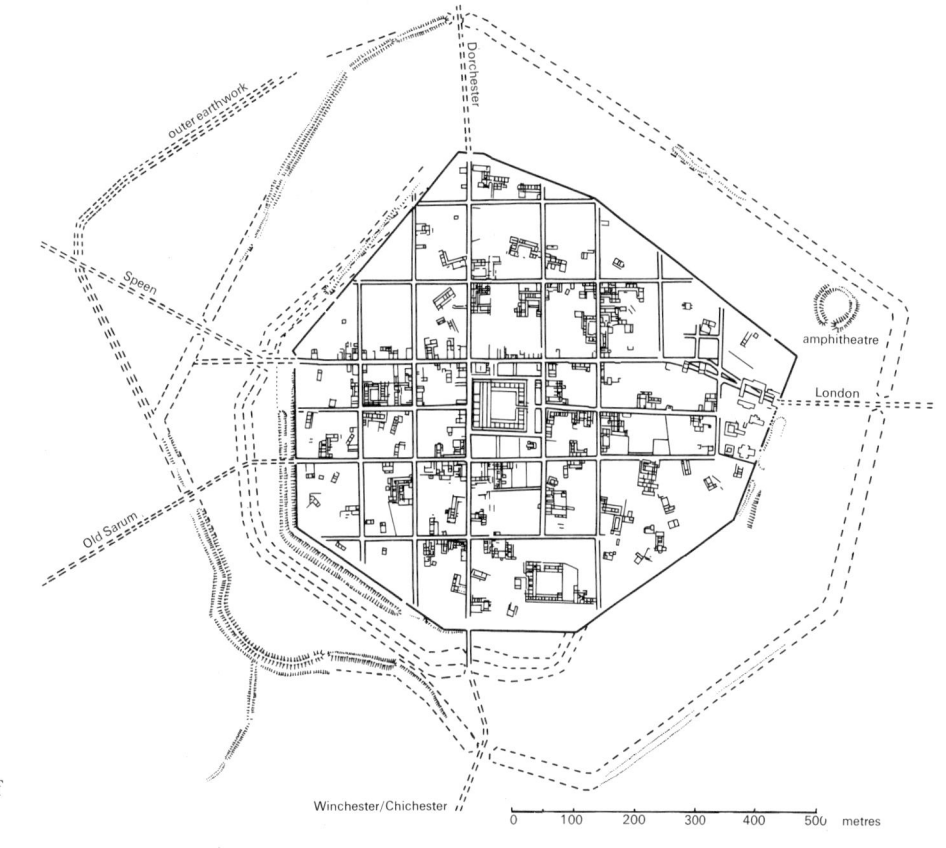

Silchester: the plan of
the Roman town.

which were rooms for shops and offices. At least one room may have been a
shrine, for it contained a dedication to Hercules. The building was decorated
with carved Bath stone, and inscriptions were carved into slabs of Purbeck
marble. A huge basilica, 71 m long, enclosed the western side of the forum,
and one of the large adjoining rooms probably contained the Romano-British
equivalent of the main council room.

Elsewhere in the town were bath-houses, wooden pipes for carrying water
and a number of temples, one of which was dedicated to Mars. Perhaps the
most interesting building of all was a small structure, just south-east of the
forum, dating to the middle of the fourth century. This is thought to be the
earliest Christian church known in Britain.

Calleva must have been much more crowded than its rather spacious plan
indicates. The early excavators probably failed to find the slight traces of
timber buildings and the damaged foundations of other structures from
which the stone had been quarried (therefore called 'robber trenches'). The
town no doubt bustled with activity, for tanners, leather-workers, blacksmiths,
carpenters, bronze and silversmiths, dyers, brewers and coopers were all
busy there.

51

Tacitus states quite openly that the Romans encouraged urbanization in Britain in order to 'persuade a people previously scattered, uncivilized and therefore prone to fight, to grow used to peace through material well-being'. One way this was done was to encourage a sense of responsibility by allowing the locals to manage some of their own affairs. Each tribal area was known as a *civitas* and had a seat of government, the equivalent of a county town or state capital. As Silchester was the tribal capital of the Atrebates, its full name was Calleva Atrebatum.

Other towns had a different status, like Gloucester which was a *colonia*, or settlement, of retired Roman soldiers. In Cicero's words they acted as a 'watch-tower and bulwark of the Roman people and a barrier of defence over and against the barbarians'. The barbarians, in Gloucester's case, were the troublesome Welsh. Lincoln, Colchester and possibly York and London were the other *coloniae* in Britain.

There were many lesser towns in Roman Britain, the character of which may be difficult to judge. Quite a few had defensive ramparts constructed around them in the second century which were later replaced by walls, and there has been a tendency on the part of archaeologists to assume a true Roman town must be walled. Some local market settlements probably had many of the characteristics of towns yet remained without defences. At Kingscote in Gloucestershire, for example, buildings cover 20 hectares. The areas outside town walls have also tended to be neglected by excavators, although they may be an urban extension of the town itself, excluded only because of military priorities when the walls were built. On the other hand, one of the most impressive defence systems in Roman Britain, the 4.5 m thick walls at Gatcombe near Bristol, has recently been shown by its latest excavator Professor Keith Branigan to enclose not a town at all but a villa.

During the 350 years of Roman rule in Britain urban settlements became well established, but have they left much impression on our modern towns? A few names are preserved—Isca Dumnoniorum is now known as Exeter, Venta Belgarum as Winchester, Londinium as London, and Eboracum first became Eforwic, 'place of the boar', a Danish pun, and was then shortened to York. Little remains to be seen nowadays of the once impressive Roman public buildings. Remarkably, in the centre of Leicester the Jewry Wall, part of a Roman bath-house, survives. More common are fragments of Roman town wall at York, Lincoln, Canterbury and Chester, or simply a change in ground level along the line of the defences.

More impressive are the surviving gateways, such as the Balkerne Gate at Colchester. Mortimer Wheeler examined this site in 1917, adopting the novel method of digging by candlelight in the basement of the King's Head public house next door. More recently excavators have found traces of the Roman town's water-pipes and a water-tower by the Balkerne Gate—a highly appropriate discovery, as visitors to Colchester can hardly fail to notice the huge Victorian water-tower which stands close by.

The Lower West Gate
of Roman Lincoln. The
road into the city runs
between two towers,
constructed in the 4th
century AD. The narrow
foundations which
cross the entrance are
the remains of the
2nd-century city walls.

We have said that relatively few Roman structures survive to the present day, but the shape and streets of Roman towns still influence the daily life of many places. The walls and defences around towns, such as Gloucester, York and Winchester, remained as a major barrier and constraint on later town planning. In an era before the bulldozer the removal of such large amounts of material was not feasible. In the fifth century AD most Roman towns probably ceased to function as urban places in the sense that we have discussed, though occupation may have continued. Their streets became disused, buildings collapsed, and even the walls and stone gateways were used as quarries. But as the towns began to come back to life in the later Saxon period, the inhabitants were hemmed in by the old defence line, and the original gateways were the only gaps. Consequently, a cross-shaped street pattern, linking the four gates, tended to be adopted on or very close to the original Roman streets.

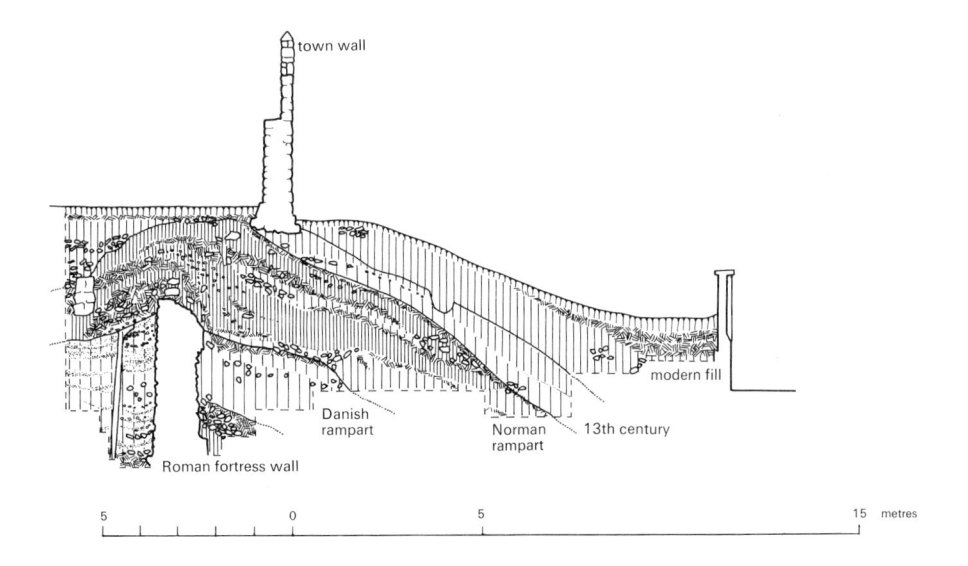

York: the superimposed
layers of the town's
Roman, Danish and
medieval defences.

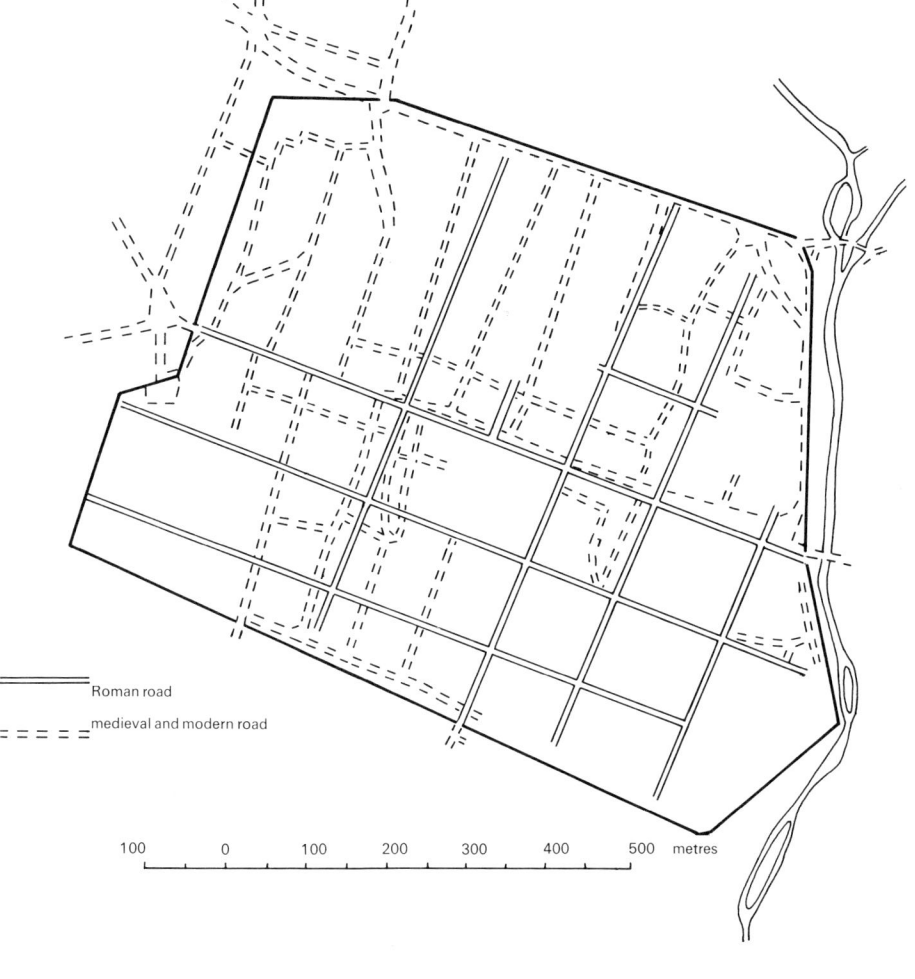

Roman road

medieval and modern road

100   0   100   200   300   400   500 metres

Winchester: Roman and
medieval street plan.

At Gloucester the North, South and East Gates are still in use, their streets
meeting at The Cross, just north of the original forum. Chichester, Exeter and
Dorchester, Dorset, among other places, show this same pattern.

Excavations at Winchester have taught us to be cautious about assuming a
cross or grid of streets implies continuity from Roman times. We now know
that the street pattern there was the creation of Alfred the Great or his im-
mediate successors. It used to be thought that after the Romans abandoned
Britain in AD 410 the towns rapidly collapsed before the Saxon onslaught.
The Saxon poem 'The Ruin' probably describes the town of Bath:

> *Splendid this rampart is, though fate destroyed it,*
> *The city buildings fell apart, the works*
> *Of giants crumble. Tumbled are the towers,*
> *Ruined the roofs, and broken the barred gate,*
> *Frost in the plaster, all the ceilings gape*
> *Torn and collapsed and eaten up by age.*

54

This rather Gothic picture of ruin and desolation needs to be modified slightly in the light of recent research.

There is evidence that occupation continued in some towns: Dorchester, Oxfordshire, and Canterbury have Saxon huts alongside the Roman streets; St Germanus was received by civic dignitaries at Verulamium in 429; and the water system was still functioning about 450. At Wroxeter painstaking excavation by Philip Barker and an army of patient trowellers has shown that substantial timber buildings were constructed in the fifth century over the rubble of the Roman masonry buildings. At Exeter's Cathedral Green on the site of the aptly named Victorian edifice, St Mary Major, a basilica building was reconstructed in the fifth century AD with reused stone and rubble. The builders seem to have forgotten how to make mortar, for they added clay and water to old mortar—and got mud! The Saxons took Exeter in the seventh century, but Britons are recorded as still living there 300 years later. They were ejected by Athelstan, but the quarter they had occupied was known as *Britayne* until the thirteenth century.

Obviously, only large-scale and careful excavation will throw further light on the complex problem of the earliest British and English towns. We must return to Winchester, where the largest campaign of urban excavation in Europe has taken place. Between 1961 and 1971 Martin Biddle and his team meticulously peeled away the layers from 11,612 sq m of the walled area, a large amount, but in fact less than 2 per cent of the total. They showed that urban life ceased at Winchester after about AD 450. Yet pagan Saxon settlements and cemeteries cluster around the town, perhaps indicating that Saxon rulers, descendants of mercenaries imported by the Roman and British administration, were occupying the old site.

A picture seems to be emerging of a place not totally abandoned at the end of the Roman period, no longer functioning as a town, but still the centre of political authority. This secular authority attracted the emissaries of the early Church. In 648 King Cenwalh founded the Church of St Peter and St Paul in Winchester, later called the Old Minster and seat of the bishop of Wessex.

In addition to the presence of the political and ecclesiastical authorities excavation at Brook Street produced evidence for a third class of occupants. A small seventh-century cemetery included one burial with gold, garnet and silver pendants and rings belonging to a person of some wealth. Nearby were the foundations of a small stone building—very unusual in this era of timber —a structure designed to be secure, because within were fragments of gold and a touchstone, the stock in trade of the assayer. This part of Winchester is likely to have been a private estate or enclosure—the original meaning of the word *burh*. A fourth element in the Saxon settlement is suggested by the occurrence of an early name, *Ceap Straet*, or Market Street, the same word which survives today in London's Cheapside. We have, then, in Winchester evidence for three classes of occupants as well as a market. In the seventh century it seems that Winchester was emerging as an English town.

It used to be thought that the reoccupation of Roman towns could be explained in terms of geographical determinism, that they were good sites from the point of view of communications or defence. This can equally be said of many places that never became towns at all. Archaeological evidence is gradually accumulating at Winchester, Dorchester (Oxfordshire), Abingdon, Canterbury, York, St Albans, Exeter and Carlisle that there has been *continuity* of settlement from the Roman period or even earlier. Particularly interesting are churches, urban, suburban and rural; more and more are proving to be on the sites of Roman buildings. Coincidence? Or was St Augustine's impact less revolutionary than is usually thought?

In the late ninth century King Alfred instigated a major programme of town building with defended centres which would provide security from the Danes for the population of Wessex. We have a list of these places in a document written about 919 and known as the *Burghal Hidage*. Excavation at Winchester has thrown new light on these Saxon towns. The grid apparent in the modern street plan is not the responsibility of the symmetrically-minded Romans as once believed; it was constructed on the orders of Alfred. Nearly nine kilometres of streets were laid out in a regular pattern and surfaced with 8,000 tonnes of flint cobbles. One street, when excavated, had been resurfaced six times. Near the bottom of this sequence of layers were found a penny of Edward the Elder, who died in 925, and an Arab coin of about AD 898.

Other towns in Wessex originated as Saxon burhs. A regular, planned lay-out of the ninth and tenth century can best be seen at Wareham, Dorset, Wallingford and Oxford. But Alfred may not have been such a great innovator, for recent work at Hereford, in Saxon Mercia, suggests other kingdoms were founding planned towns at the same time or even earlier.

The burhs were designed essentially as defensive sites. Early Winchester, we have seen, functioned as some kind of administrative and ecclesiastical centre. So is there any evidence of early Saxon towns devoted essentially to those other important activities—trade and industry? The county in which Winchester lies, Hampshire, takes its name from a town which no longer exists. In the last century clay-digging and the construction of terraced houses in the north-east suburbs of Southampton, close by a tidal lagoon of the river Itchen, produced many finds that indicated this was the site of the county's eponymous settlement—Hamwih. About 950 Hamwih was more or less abandoned in favour of the new site of Southampton on a plateau of gravel between the rivers Test and Itchen. Perhaps silting in the shallow lagoon made the old harbour unsuitable for the increasingly large merchant ships. Conditions for modern excavation are difficult with limited space available and much destroyed by quarrying, but there have been tantalizing glimpses of a flourishing Saxon trading centre. Most interesting is the possibility of a grid of streets as early as the seventh century with houses at the front of tenements and wells, latrines and rubbish pits behind. The local industries included iron-smelting, smithing, lead, bronze and silverworking, potting, textile

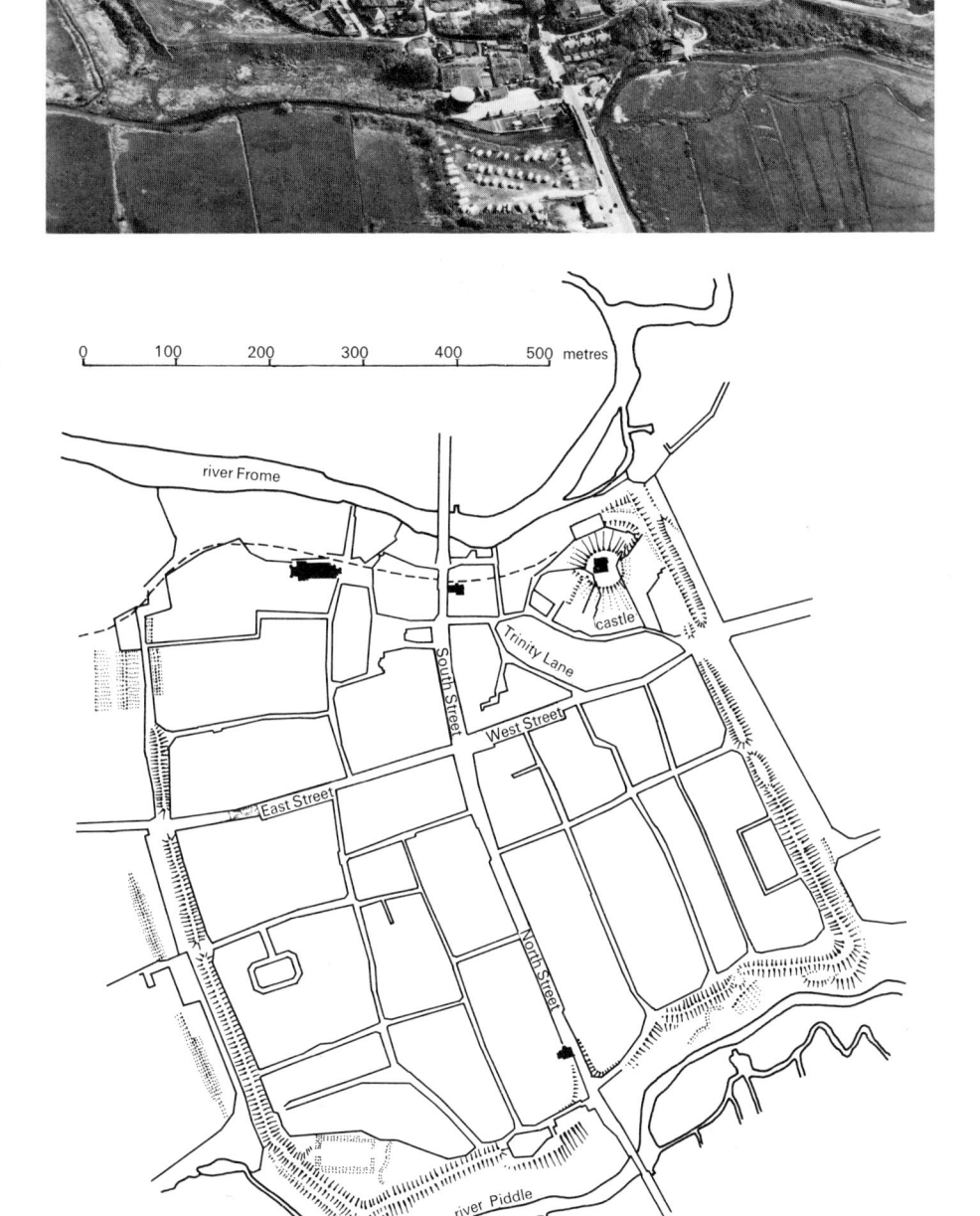

Wareham, Dorset. The rectangular outline of the Saxon burh constructed at the time of Alfred and its internal grid of streets is still visible in the modern town plan.

Viking York. The foundations of these timber buildings have been preserved in the airless, waterlogged ground below the modern city. These conditions provide archaeologists with a vast amount of organic material and evidence which rarely survives elsewhere in Britain.

production and manufacture of wood and bone objects. There was a mint in the town, and overseas traders imported Continental pottery, glass and quern-stones.

Winchester and Hamwih seem to have been closely linked as the political and commercial centres of Wessex. It is possible that each of the other major Saxon kingdoms had a similar port of trade, and it has been suggested by Martin Biddle that Fordwich, Sandwich, Dover in Kent and Ipswich in Suffolk would repay archaeological investigation. Certainly, the Danish and Viking trading centres of York and Dublin are proving to be two of the most exciting of current excavation projects.

We have stressed before the great advantage of sites where preservation is exceptional. In some countries, such as Egypt or Peru, the arid conditions may lead to the survival of papyrus, textiles or even human bodies. In Britain dryness may be impossible, but waterlogging is not.

At York's Lloyds Bank site archaeologists found a 5 m deep deposit of waterlogged material, a treasure-house of mud, laden with biological information. Less than fastidious Anglo-Danish leather-workers had occupied the tenements, throwing down layers of rushes on the sodden floor. Their working conditions were only too obvious from the insects that were found in this mess; they were identical to those that live in compost heaps. To make matters worse the hair and fat from raw hides had been thrown into a corner

58

of the room and left to seethe with maggots, whose puparia were discovered in the excavation. The inhabitants of York seem not to have changed much 400 years later. In October 1332 Edward III demanded that they clean up their streets because of the 'abominable smell abounding in the said city more than in any other city of the realm from dung and manure and other filth and dirt wherewith the streets and lanes are here filled and obstructed'.

These little difficulties of drainage are a godsend to archaeologists, and excavations at Coppergate have produced the finest sequence of preserved Viking timber buildings in the country. Work at York seems destined to put the Scandinavian impact on British urbanization into something like a proper perspective for the first time.

In a short chapter like this it is impossible to do credit to the subject of urban archaeology. The last decade has seen a great boom in the amount of excavation, and most of the results remain unpublished and undigested. The effects have been most rewarding in the earlier periods, though traces of Saxon or Scandinavian occupation remain tantalizingly scarce in many towns. Later disturbances so often destroy the underlying layers. Attention is at last being paid to the long-neglected subject of church archaeology. Biddle has excavated six of Winchester's fifty-seven parish churches and shown how complex their development can be. Similarly, at Oxford work in the redundant eighteenth-century church of All Saints located an underlying medieval church, a Saxon building and property boundary. Most ambitious of all has been the difficult excavation under York Minster which was conducted as part of the restoration programme between 1966 and 1971. One of the most dramatic finds here was a toppled column of the Roman basilica underlying the minster. This would not have been too surprising in itself, except that the basilica appears to have been standing until the ninth or tenth century AD.

It is not necessary to dig to study the development of a town; the townscape itself holds many clues to its origin and growth. The pattern of streets, the type of buildings and topography are there to be seen in historic towns. We must try to visualize the setting that confronted the first settlers: where are the highest points, the steepest slopes, streams, and areas liable to flood? All these may influence the topography of the present town but be barely perceptible to the busy man in the street, now that they are masked by buildings, or in the case of streams, like the Fleet in London, channelled into pipes beneath his feet. Are there any relict features which influence the modern scene— ancient boundaries, for example? Why are the streets laid out in a particular way? Is the church unusually large? Why so many alleyways or pubs? Every town is unique, an endless source of speculation, and beneath the streets lies the accumulated evidence of the past.

It would require a whole book to describe adequately the richness of the townscape. Fortunately, a very good one has recently appeared called *The Landscape of Towns* (1976) by Mick Aston and James Bond, who combine the skills of the historical geographer and the archaeologist. They emphasize

As in York, waterlogging can preserve ancient timbers remarkably well along the City of London's river frontage. Recent excavations at Trig Lane and other sites are revealing the Roman and medieval wharves of London.

the potential of the visible above-ground evidence, which can tell us so much when combined with a knowledge of the historical development of towns, an eye for urban patterns and some skill in vernacular architecture.

It is always worth looking at the plan of a town to see if it has a characteristic shape. Not only the Romans and Saxons used the grid pattern; the Normans were also fond of it. Ludlow, New Sarum and New Winchelsea are the classic examples. But just in case you are inclined to think that every English town ought to look like a chess-board, it should be pointed out that by far the majority of new Norman towns were not regularly laid out at all.

60

Even when they were planned as a unity such places can demonstrate a subtle use of the site; the medieval planner was much more responsive to the natural lie of the land than his rather dogmatic Roman predecessor. For obvious reasons the new Norman rulers of the eleventh century often imposed a dominating castle as the focal point of their towns. Conway, founded in 1284 by Edward I, is a good example of the interplay of defensive needs and commercial common sense. The grid pattern of the streets is not rigid but staggered, creating a pleasanter urban environment. The motivation was principally financial, however, for in this way the maximum number of burgage plots could be placed on the main street, raising a correspondingly large harvest of rents.

Right An 18th-century view of Conway Castle, Caernarvonshire. Such prints can provide the urban archaeologist with interesting evidence.

Below Conway: the elements of the medieval planned town and its underlying relief.

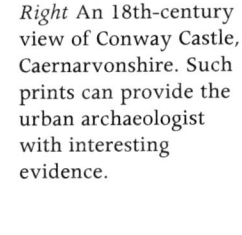

Conway estuary

Conway estuary

▦ church	▭ meridian street systems
▥ staggered parallel street system	▨ harbour

▦ later extensions	⊶ Conway Castle
▧ market colonization	

0   100   200   300   400   500   600   700   800   900   1,000 metres

After the initial phase of Norman military control, commercial needs became paramount in most towns, and so the market became the heart. The Saxon burh had no specially designated open space, simply the central intersection of streets. The market-place, though, is characteristic of medieval towns, often a triangle of land outside a castle or abbey but in some cases dominating the shape of the whole town. The earliest known spindle-shaped market, of about 1130, is at Newport in Shropshire, while at Thame in 1219 the Bishop of Lincoln had the main Oxford to Aylesbury road diverted by one mile to encourage visitors into his new market. The space available for the flocks of animals, tradesmen and customers is still obvious, although the Bishop tried to get the best of all possible worlds. In 1221 there were complaints that he 'made on the King's highway in the Forum of Thame an encroachment where he raised houses to increase his rent, to the length of 100 feet in all'. In many towns the once spacious markets have been infilled, often as temporary stalls evolved into permanent structures.

Thame, Oxfordshire, with its fine spindle-shaped medieval market and long, narrow burgage plots. The island of buildings represents late and post-medieval infilling of the market.

The Shambles at York with its jettied buildings overhanging a mere passage is generally assumed to be typical of medieval streets. Certain towns like Tewkesbury and Nottingham were notoriously crowded, restricted for space by rivers in one case and its own open fields in the other. Consequently, houses were built behind one another and linked by alleyways. On the other hand, the spaciousness of Thame is a reminder that medieval streets could be quite generous in their proportions. At Stratford the streets were 15 m wide, and the main one was 27 m across. At right angles to the medieval street burgage plots were laid out. They were generally long and narrow to give the maximum number of street frontages. Those visible in the photograph of Thame are large, 195 m by 18 m, but in other towns they could be as narrow as 3 m. The buildings stood at the front of the tenements at right angles to the street with, excavators so often find, privies and rubbish pits behind. The property boundaries can be extremely persistent, and the arrangement of burgage plots is still visible in many towns.

All Saints' Church, Oxford. Excavations below the floor of this 18th-century church revealed the foundations of its medieval predecessor and a building dating to the late Saxon period. The church has now been converted into a library for Lincoln College. Important archaeological evidence is often lost when redundant churches are subject to conversion.

Archaeologists in towns have tended to concentrate on the below-ground evidence, and at Winchester, Northampton and Oxford blocks of tenements have been excavated. Ten stone houses dating back to the thirteenth century were uncovered at St Peter's Street, Northampton, generally about 8 m by 4 m, their long axis along the street, with two rooms on the ground floor. The yards at the back were, of course, full of the ubiquitous rubbish pits, so beloved of urban archaeologists. These medieval buildings had been reduced to their foundations; standing ones have in comparison been neglected.

Below The west front of Exeter Cathedral dominates the superbly preserved remains of the Roman legionary bath-house. The pillars of tiles supported the floor so that warm air could circulate beneath. The masonry running diagonally across the picture, in front of the site hut, is the foundation of the Victorian church of St Mary Major.

Right The Abbot's House, Butcher Row, Shrewsbury. This house, which is still standing, was built before 1485. Archaeology is three-dimensional, and the evidence can be above our heads in existing buildings as well as beneath our feet in buried layers. Recent excavations opposite the Abbot's House show that there is Saxon occupation below.

Urban archaeology should start at the rooftops and work down, but too often the buildings which survive are ignored until they are demolished. Alternatively, buildings may be gutted internally under the guidance of an 'enlightened' planning department, aware of its responsibility to the street-scape. But, as in a Hollywood film set, behind the façade is an historical vacuum. Buildings can be deceptive: many Georgian frontages conceal half-timbered structures of much earlier date, and it is necessary to look at the back, inside and in the roof to see what is going on. A house I lived in myself, in Abingdon, was listed simply as eighteenth century. In fact, behind its Queen Anne façade was a sixteenth-century wing, and sandwiched between this and the main block was a tiny fifteenth-century cottage with original ogee windows. Under the cottage was a cellar which might have been as early as the thirteenth century.

Students of urban archaeology are becoming more broadminded. The importance and interest of post-medieval towns, industrial archaeology and nineteenth-century artisans' housing is being realized, although rather too late to save much of the primary evidence. At Bath, Britain's greatest spa in the Roman period and the eighteenth century, much of the lower-class housing has already been bulldozed. John Wood's Royal Crescent may be an architectural jewel but it is in danger of shining in aristocratic isolation.

Town-bashing is a long-established British tradition, and the political journalist and essayist William Cobbett (1763–1835), who despised London as 'the Great Wen', was one of its most colourful practitioners. To him Bath was where 'East India plunderers, West India floggers, English tax-gorgers, together with gluttons, drunkards and debauchers of all descriptions, female as well as male, resort, at the suggestion of silently laughing quacks, in the hope of getting rid of the bodily consequences of their manifold sins and iniquities'. Somehow, though, if Cobbett were alive, I think he might have got to like the place and appreciate the rich heritage of a town where all walks of life are represented in its physical structure.

The City of London. St Paul's and some less illustrious architecture rise above the complex archaeological layers of the General Post Office site.

5 Approaches to the past

The distinctions between archaeology, history, geography and other subjects can become very blurred: this is as it should be. The enquiry into the human past—history in its widest sense—involves using many different techniques and every piece of evidence that is available, whether it be written documents, inscriptions on stone, coins, potsherds, animal bones or the landscape itself. Unfortunately, words, particularly labels, can build barriers as easily as destroy them. Academic specialists called archaeologists, historians or anthropologists are inclined to wall themselves up within the limited confines of their own particular cells.

It has often been pointed out that increasing specialization makes communication much more difficult, yet in recent years there have been increasingly frequent calls for 'total archaeology', combining all the sources of evidence. This may sound like a pious hope, but archaeologists need to understand the evidence used by their colleagues in related fields, its potential and its limitations. Equally, many historians feel ill at ease in the strange world of the excavation report, do not know how to handle the unfamiliar evidence and, to be honest, do not get much help. On the other hand, botanists and anthropologists are often inclined to ignore the dimension of the past altogether and work only in the present. In the United States similar problems arise, except that there archaeology is taught within anthropology departments. As North American archaeology is almost by definition prehistoric archaeology, the influence of historians has been minimal; instead, the subject is seen as a branch of the social sciences. In the words of Gordon Willey and Philip Phillips, 'American archaeology is anthropology or it is nothing.' Students of pre-Columbian America have no documentation to provide any sort of framework on which to hang their archaeological evidence. Consequently, until recently they have tended to cling to that constructed by anthropologists working on American Indian societies. American archaeologists felt themselves the Cinderellas of the anthropological world, scraping among the cinders while their colleagues in the mainstream made the really important contributions. In the early 60s some American archaeologists began to flex their muscles. Announcing themselves as New Archaeologists, they proclaimed the scientific validity of archaeology as practised by them and its ability to make original contributions to mainstream

anthropology. Out of this ferment many new ideas and techniques have emerged, often, unfortunately, couched in an excessive amount of jargon. The sort of soul-searching which has gone on in archaeology over the last ten years is healthy and beneficial providing it leads to the demolition of the cell walls and the establishment of common ground. There is always a danger that instead more barriers will go up around cells of academic sectarianism, led by high priests of obscurity.

We have already discussed the early development of European archaeology and the reliance on historical models. Druids from the pages of Caesar, stock biblical characters and Homeric heroes were used to explain archaeological problems because, at the time, there was little else to go on. In more recent years historically-minded archaeologists have had genuine success in answering specific questions and fleshing out the bones of a sparse documentary narrative.

A classic example of this kind of work is that carried out by Sir Ian Richmond at the hill-fort of Hod Hill, Dorset. In AD 43 four Roman legions and auxiliaries, altogether about 40,000 men, sailed from Boulogne under their commander, Aulus Plautius. Their object was to conquer Britain. We know

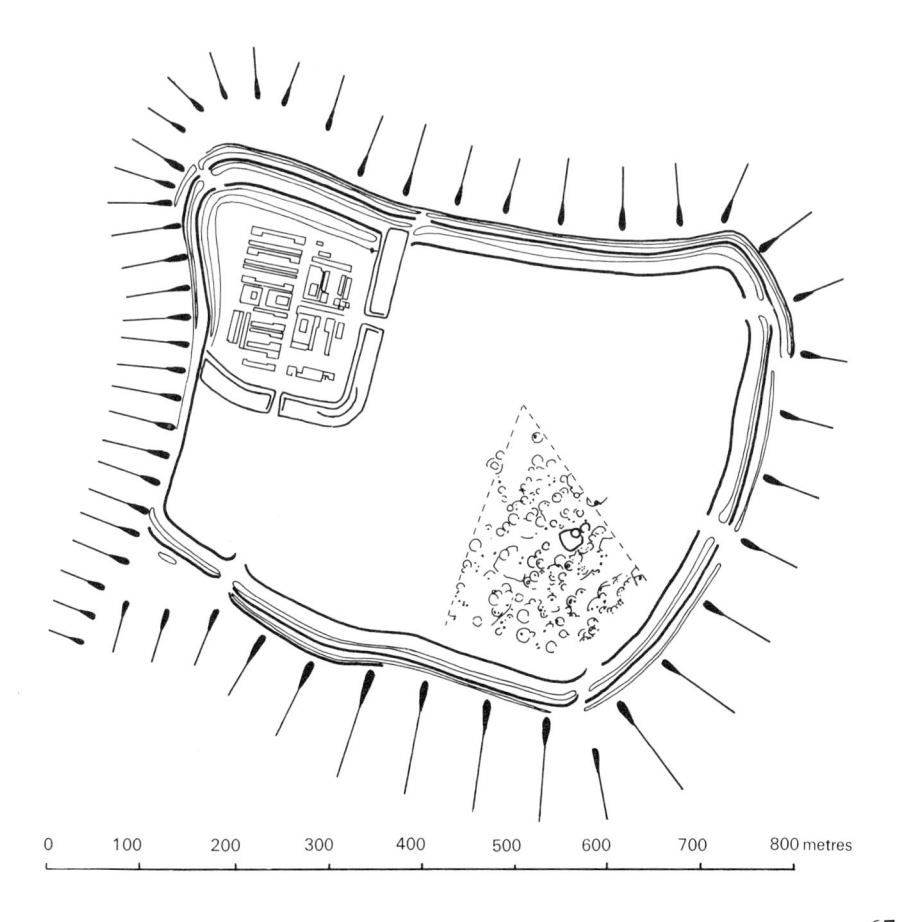

Hod Hill, Dorset. The earthworks of Iron Age hut circles survive in a triangle of unploughed land. The Roman fort sits in the north-west corner of the hill-fort.

0	100	200	300	400	500	600	700	800 metres

67

this much from Roman literary sources, principally the writings of Dio Cassius, Tacitus and Suetonius. But their accounts are relatively thin; there are many things we would like to know which they do not tell us. Some of the important parts of their work have been lost, and we have to consider their natural bias and any simple mistakes or deliberate errors.

The activities of one of the four legions, *Legio 11*, are better known than the rest because its legate, Vespasian, later became Emperor. Suetonius in his *Lives* says that Vespasian with his legion 'proceeded to Britain where he fought thirty battles, subjugated two warlike tribes, and captured more than twenty towns, besides the entire Isle of Wight'. And that is about all. Suetonius obviously did not think the conquest of Britain was particularly important. Ian Richmond did, however, and he was particularly interested in this phrase 'captured twenty towns'. It was generally agreed among Classical historians and archaeologists that *Legio 11*, operated, at this time, in the south-west of Britain. This fitted the statement that the Isle of Wight was among the con-quered territories. Richmond believed that one of the warlike tribes was likely to be the Durotriges, who lived in the area that is now Dorset and south Somerset, and that the 'twenty towns' were to be sought among their imposing hill-forts.

Hod Hill seemed a likely candidate because in one corner of the hill-fort a Roman fort had been constructed. The obvious context for this event was the early years of the Conquest, when Roman troops would have been stationed there to keep the truculent Durotriges in order. Richmond tackled the hill-fort with these specific questions in mind and answered them in his extremely readable excavation report.

Inside the hill-fort many circular houses could be seen, and the archaeolo-gists concentrated their excavation on the largest of these. The area around this was found to be littered with Roman ballista bolts, the iron points from spear-like missiles which were projected from a crossbow-like machine. Richmond vividly reconstructed the course of events—where the ballistae had been set up and how a heavy barrage had been directed at the 'Chieftain's Hut', no doubt forcing the defenders on the ramparts to keep their heads down while the Roman troops assaulted the gates. After the capture of the Celtic settlement, the defences were slighted and the Roman fort erected. In his account of the Roman fort Richmond skilfully married the archaeological evidence with his knowledge of Roman military history to produce a smooth narrative; indeed, Hod Hill is a most readable excavation report.

It would be ungracious to deny the importance of Sir Ian Richmond's work at Hod Hill, but many archaeologists have criticized his approach. The report has little to say about the Iron Age hill-fort, the structure, size and economy of the community that lived there or its relationship to the sur-rounding area. It concentrates on one event in the life of the Celtic com-munity—in fact, its death. Richmond could quite justifiably reply that like a good researcher he wanted to know the answers to certain questions, chose his

Right The so-called Chieftain's Hut at Hod Hill and the position of the Roman ballista bolts with which it was bombarded by Vespasian's army. One of the two circular huts is surrounded by an enclosure.

Below A view of the adjacent hill-forts on Hod Hill and Hambledon Hill in Dorset by the archaeologist Heywood Sumner in his distinctive style. The Roman fort can be seen in the corner of Hod's Celtic defences in the foreground of the picture.

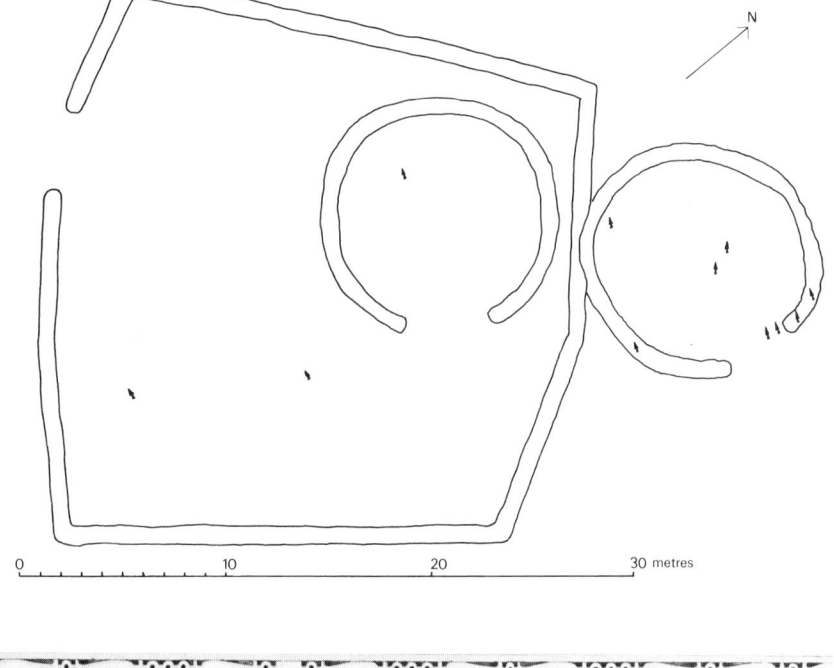

A BIRD'S EYE VIEW OF HOD HILL & OF HAMBLEDON HILL. H.S. 1913

Maiden Castle, Dorset, and Sir Mortimer Wheeler's excavations in the complex entrance of this imposing hill-fort. The grid of trenches is characteristic of Wheeler's systematic and disciplined method of digging, though now regarded as over rigid. In the background are the foundations of a Romano-Celtic temple, built inside the hill-fort after its abandonment.

site, carried out his experiment and published his conclusions. His critics would reply that he may have presented his conclusions but he did not present his results. Richmond did not burden his report with data; instead, he presented a free-flowing narrative with his conclusions neatly packaged. The reader could take them or leave them but he or she could not analyse the evidence or the underlying assumptions. The critics could, and did, say that this emphasis on 'text-aided' archaeology was painting the subject into a corner, making it a subsidiary of documentary history and neglecting the two million years or so of human existence in which there were no literary sources around to give the archaeologist a leg-up.

There is no denying the popular appeal of 'personality' archaeology. Mortimer Wheeler said that 'dead archaeology is the driest dust that blows' and that 'the past is about people'. Like Richmond, one of the people he was interested in was Vespasian, and he also found evidence of this unwelcome visitor among the Durotriges. Maiden Castle, in spite of its colossal ramparts, fell to the second legion with apparently little difficulty. Skulls slashed by

swords and a skeleton with a Roman ballista bolt embedded in its spinal column are a vivid illustration of the efficiency of Vespasian's troops. Wheeler was fond not only of digging-up 'people' in general but 'personalities' in particular. Probably for this reason he carried out excavations at Stanwick, in Yorkshire, where a defended site of 7 hectares was increased in size to 295 hectares some time after AD 70. Wheeler believed this to be the headquarters of Venutius, husband of Cartimandua, Queen of the Brigantes, who objected to his wife's policy of appeasement and so broke away from her and rebelled against Rome. Again the principal aim of this excavation was to enlarge upon a particular historical incident and illuminate an historical personality.

Excavation does not always confirm and supplement ideas based on historical evidence. It would be unfair to classify Leslie Alcock's work at Cadbury Castle in Somerset simply as 'personality' archaeology, but the site's association with King Arthur is what attracted the attention of the Press. This hill-fort also seemed a likely candidate for the attentions of our old friend Vespasian, and signs were in fact found of an attack by Roman troops. In this case the dating evidence, in particular a series of brooches, suggested that the siege took place twenty years after Vespasian's perambulation around the south-west. If this is so, then the historical sources tell us nothing about these particular troubles. Similarly, at Castle Hill, Almondbury, excavation has shown that the site was not the capital of Cartimandua, Queen of the Brigantes, as often thought, because by her time the hill-fort had long been abandoned.

If 'Vespasian slept here' archaeology has gone out of fashion, that is not to say that there is or ever has been too much co-operation between historians and archaeologists. There is still a general lack of understanding between the two disciplines, particularly about the shortcomings of their respective evidence.

The most promising field in which historians and archaeologists are working together is in the study of towns. Martin Biddle has stressed that at Winchester whereas the archaeological excavations reveal 'the facts of daily life' the documents mainly deal with legal, administrative and financial matters. The two types of evidence together present a much fuller picture than would either considered in isolation. Co-operation is also developing in the study of medieval villages. The most tenacious piece of work is at Wharram Percy in Yorkshire, where Maurice Beresford and John Hurst, as historian and archaeologist, have been studying the deserted village since 1950. Beresford has no illusions about the evidence: 'On many occasions a working historian is brought up against the sad fact that in respect of documentary evidence his Dark Age may extend far beyond whatever point is conventionally taken as the end of the "Dark Ages" and the dawn of medieval light . . . an historian may have cause to bemoan the paucity or absence of documents which he can summon to his aid. But when he surveys the much more severe restraints on the activities of the research archaeologist he may pause to count his blessings.'

Castle Hill, Almondbury, West Yorkshire. The conveniently defensive site of the Iron Age hill-fort was utilized for the motte and bailey castle (the mound at the right of the hill-fort) following the Norman Conquest. The tower inside the Norman Castle was built to commemorate Queen Victoria's diamond jubilee. The hill-fort has often been claimed to be the headquarters of Queen Cartimandua of the Brigantes, but excavation has shown that the site had long been abandoned by the 1st century AD.

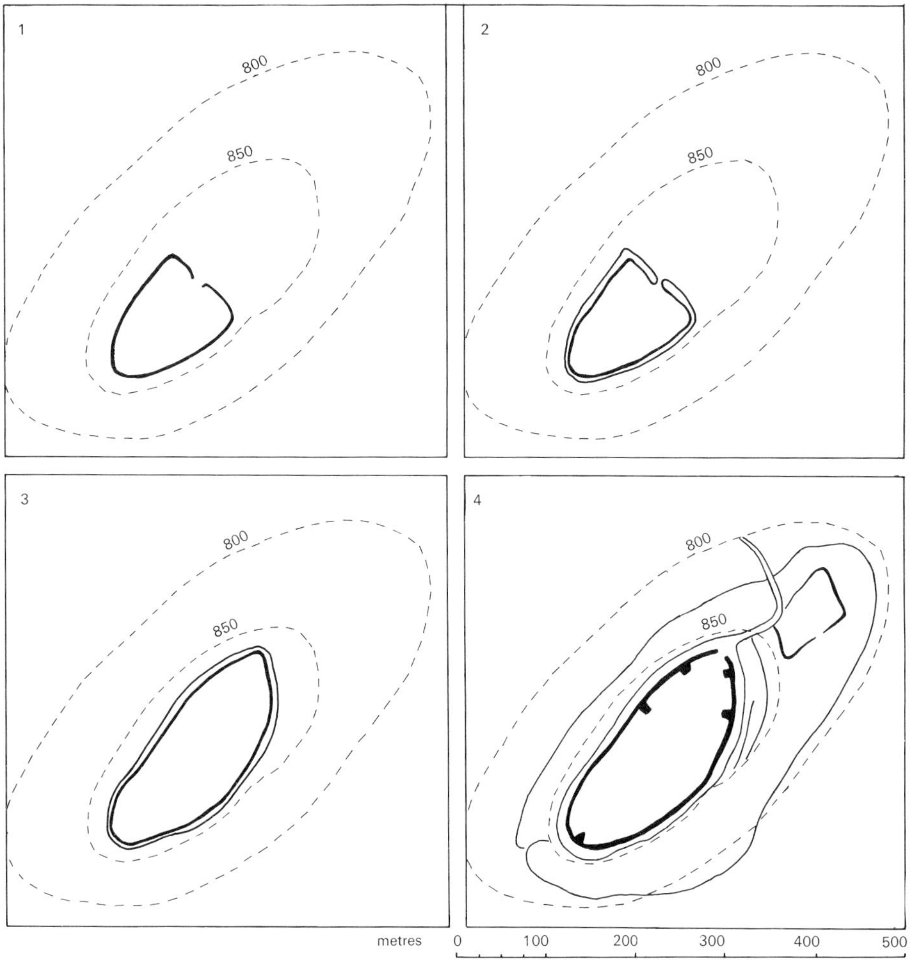

Castle Hill, Almondbury, West Yorkshire. The hill-fort had a long and complex life, and the plans show its evolution during the first millennium BC, culminating in the burning of the ramparts in the 5th century BC.

1

800

850

2

800

850

3

800

850

4

800

850

metres   0   100   200   300   400   500

Other historians, less familiar with the methods and problems of archaeology, may accept statements at face value or ignore the results altogether. In 1922 E. T. Leeds carried out the first excavation of a pagan Anglo-Saxon village at Sutton Courtenay, Berkshire. Historical evidence suggested that Saxon villages had substantial timber buildings or halls as their main dwellings. What Leeds found was a collection of small, miserable-looking huts, their floors sunken into the ground. The idea then circulated that the early Saxon settlers in Britain lived in glorified dog kennels, and this generalization is still repeated in historians' accounts of early Saxon England.

But what were the facts? Leeds was not conducting a formal, scientific excavation; he was doing his best to salvage evidence in a gravel pit. Judging from contemporary photographs, the conditions were pretty appalling, and the area badly disturbed by the quarrying activities. The sunken huts, cut 60–90 cm into the gravel subsoil, were easy to see because they appeared as large, black squares of soil in the yellow gravel. The timber halls, familiar on the Continent, were usually supported by posts only a few centimetres in diameter, which may or may not have penetrated the subsoil. In fact, Leeds did find some lines of post-holes, but the conditions were totally inappropriate for the recovery of house plans.

Drayton/Sutton Courtenay, Oxfordshire: the irregular, branching crop marks indicate frost cracks caused in the last glaciation. Most of the other marks are man-made, such as the parallel lines of a late Neolithic *cursus* and the circular ditches around ploughed-out Bronze Age barrows. In the centre are six rectangular features, probably Saxon houses. Saxon settlements have only recently been identified from aerial photography.

More recently, carefully conducted excavations with better facilities and conditions at sites like Chalton, Hampshire, have recovered plans of the sort of building historical sources suggest existed. One thinks, for example, of the words spoken by a thegn of Edwin, King of Northumberland, and recorded by Bede: 'Your Majesty, when we compare the present life of man with that time of which we have no knowledge, it seems to me like the swift flight of a lone sparrow through the banqueting-hall where you sit in the winter months to dine with your thanes and counsellors. Inside there is a comforting fire to warm the room, outside, the wintry storms of snow and rain are raging. The sparrow flies swiftly in through one door of the hall, and out through the other.'

We can see what was meant by this description of two doors, because Edwin's royal seat of ad Gefrin has been found and excavated at Yeavering in Northumberland. The main hall had two doorways opposite one another in its long axis and fits perfectly the story of the sparrow. On a lesser scale Chalton's

Chalton, Hampshire: the foundation slots of a Saxon house, similar to those visible as crop marks at Sutton Courtenay in Oxfordshire. It has central entrances in its long sides and conforms to the description of a hall in Bede's *Historia Ecclesiastica*. The scored lines in the chalk are caused by continual ploughing of the site.

houses have similar plans. Even the original home of the sunken hut, Sutton Courtenay, now has a group of large, impressive halls, showing in aerial photographs, apparently also with central doors. The sunken huts can, at last, be seen for what they are—the community's work sheds.

It is sometimes said that because archaeological evidence is 'unconscious' evidence it is less prone to inbuilt bias than the written word. When we write, we may exaggerate, tell lies or simply get our facts wrong, but when we throw out the rubbish or build a house, we bare our souls. This is a comforting thought for archaeologists but overlooks all the other problems—the inaccessibility of sites in Britain, the expense of excavation, bad excavation and interpretation, and the disappearance of most of a community's material possessions. To illustrate this last point the archaeologist Peter Addyman has called attention to a late Saxon document, *The Sagacious Reeve*, which lists the tasks, duties and possessions of the village headman:

'. . . 14. He should provide many tools for the homestead, and get many implements for the buildings: (as for instance)—

15. An axe, adze, bill, awl, plane, saw, chimbe-iron, tie-hook, auger, mattock, prise, share, coulter; and also a goad iron, scythe, sickle, weed-hook, spade, shovel, woad-dibble, barrow, besom, beetle, rake, fork, ladder, horse-comb and shears, fire-tongs, weighing-scale and many spinning-implements (such as): flax-threads, spindle, reel, yarn-winder, stoddle, weaver's beams, press, comb, carding-tool, weft, woof, wool-comb, roller, slay[?], winder with a bent handle, shuttle, seam-pegs, shears, needle, slick-stone

. . . 17. One ought to have coverings for wains, ploughing gear, harrowing tackle, and many things that I cannot now name; as well as a measure, an awl, and a flail for the threshing floor, and many implements besides; as a cauldron, leaden vessel, kettle, ladle, pan, crock, fire-dog, dishes, bowls with handles, tubs, buckets, a churn, cheese-vat, bags, baskets, crates, bushels, sieves, seed-basket, wire-sieve, hair-sieve, winnowing fans, troughs, ash-wood pails, hives, honey-bins, beer-barrels, bathing-tub, bowls, butts, dishes, vessels, cips, strainers, candle-sticks, salt-cellar, spoon-case, pepper-horn, chest, money-box, yeast-box, seats [?], foot-stools, chairs, basins, lamp, lantern, leathern-bottles, box for resin (or soap), comb, iron bin, rack for fodder, fire-guard, meal-ark, oil flask, oven-rake and dung-shovel.

18. It is toilsome to recount all that he who holds this office ought to think of; he ought never to neglect anything that may prove useful, not even a mouse-trap. . . .'

It is salutary to think that seventy-five items in the list were made largely of wood or other organic material which would only survive in exceptional circumstances. At the Saxon village of Chalton, Hampshire, the excavators found very few artefacts, as was the case at Yeavering, Northumberland, the site of the royal palace of ad Gefrin. Presumably, the King liked the

Left The bust of Christ on the floor mosaic at Hinton St Mary, Dorset. His identity is indicated by the chi-rho behind His head and the pomegranates, symbols of eternal life, on either side.

Below Christian acrostic, or word square, from Roman Cirencester incised on wall plaster. The letters form an anagram of *Pater Noster alpha et omega.*

R O T A S
O P E R A
T E N E T
A R E P O
S A T O R

Below A possible reconstruction of the inscription from the forum at Verulamium. The surviving pieces are stippled. It appears to support Tacitus' statement that Agricola actively encouraged urbanization in Britain.

place kept clean, and the lack of rubbish is no more surprising than in a modern house. The apparent poverty of a site need not reflect the real situation.

It is true, though, that archaeology can correct the focus of historians by making them aware of the limitations of their documents. Historians studying medieval villages have often worked from quite recent maps and assumed that the settlement plans they show correspond with the earlier medieval ones. Excavations at Wharram Percy and other villages reveal a kaleidoscopic scene, with houses changing axes and shifting about, roads moving, the open fields in a constant state of flux, and even the manor-house and church do not always stay in one place. In urban studies also the information supplied by documents can be supplemented by excavation. At Winchester out of fifty-seven parish churches in the town and its suburbs historical evidence suggested that only three were Saxon foundations. So far five have been excavated, and four of them proved to have Saxon origins, though only one had supporting documentary evidence.

Archaeologists working in literate periods may become directly involved with historical evidence by actually digging it up. In some parts of the world the search for buried documentary material, such as inscribed tablets, has often, unfortunately, overshadowed everything else, and other forms of evidence have suffered. In Britain the written word can appear carved in stone, inscribed on pots or plaster, set in mosaic and occasionally written on wooden tablets as at the Roman site of Chew Park, Somerset, and Vindolanda on Hadrian's Wall. Inscriptions on stone most often appear on tombstones of Roman or later date, recording the names and careers of the individuals they commemorate, and they may help the military historian to discover the location of a particular body of troops or give the social historian some idea of the cosmopolitan nature of the community in a particular place. Roman York, for example, had a Gallic priest with a Greek name married to a Sardinian woman. Inscriptions from Roman Britain also occur on public monuments, such as that from the forum at Verulamium. If this reconstruction is correct, then it provides supporting evidence for the statements of Tacitus that Agricola actively encouraged the construction of towns.

If inscriptions can be fragmentary, they can also be indecipherable. The work of Michael Ventris in the 50s on the Linear B Tablets of Crete and Greece is the best-known example of archaeological code-cracking, but Scottish archaeologists have a more frustrating task with stones inscribed in Pictish.

IMP·TITO·CAESARI·DIVI·VESPASIANI·F·VESPASIANO·AVG
PM·TR·P·VIIII·IMP·XV·COS·VII·DESIG·VIII·CENSORI·PATRI·PATRIAE
ET·CAESARI·DIVI·VESPASIANI·F·DOMITIANO·COS·VI·DESIG·VII·PRINCIPI
IVVENTVTIS·ET·OMNIVM·COLLEGIORVM·SACERDOTI
CN·IVLIO·AGRICOLA·LEGATO·AVG·PRO·PR
MVNICIPIVM·VERVLAMIVM·BASILICA·ORNATA

Memorial stone of the 6th century from Carmarthen with inscriptions in Latin and around the edge in ogham, both commemorating a certain *Votecorigas*. The ogham alphabet, the first form of writing to be used in Celtic Ireland, adapted the Latin alphabet into a rectilinear script.

The Alfred Jewel found in 1693 at North Petherton, Somerset. The enamel work design is covered by a plate of rock crystal and set in a gold frame. The jewel can be dated on stylistic grounds to the late 9th century AD but more reliably carries the inscription in Anglo-Saxon: † AELFRED MEC HEHT GEWYRCAN (Alfred had me made.) It is generally accepted that this refers to *the* King Alfred.

Only a few words of the language are known and most of them are personal names.

It is now unfashionable to call the post-Roman period the 'Dark Ages', for there are many documents belonging to the years between AD 400 and 700. But they are written in several different and difficult languages and are often very brief. Proto-historic and early historic periods may produce some written evidence, such as coins in the late Iron Age or tombstones in the post-Roman period, yet they remain to all intents and purposes prehistoric. We are then dependent on the skills of the archaeologist.

Human beings, or something like them, have been on earth for approximately two million years (some people would say longer). If we imagine this span of time as a twenty-four-hour clock, then mankind first learnt to write at three and a half minutes to midnight; the rest of the day we were illiterate. The documentary historian cannot, therefore, claim to have a monopoly of the past. The early antiquaries realized that their written sources gave them little guidance once they ventured into the darkness of prehistory. In search of explanations they turned to the so-called primitive peoples of the newly colonized lands of America. As early as 1654 John Aubrey crystallized the potential avenues of enquiry in this famous passage from *An Essay Towards the Description of the North Division of Wiltshire*:

'Let us imagine then what kind of countrie this was in the time of the ancient Britons. By the nature of the soil, which is sour woodsere land, very natural for the production of oakes especially, one may conclude that this North Division was a shady dismal wood: and the inhabitants almost as savage as the beasts whose skins were their only rainment. The language British, which for the honour of it was in those days spoken from the Orcades to Italie and Spain. The boats of the Avon (which signifies River) were basketts of twigges covered with an oxe skin: which the poore people of Wales use to this day. They call them *curricles*. Within this shire I believe there were several *Reguli* which often made war on one another: and the great ditches which run on the plaines and elsewhere so many miles (not unlikely) their boundaries: and withall served for defence against the incursions of their enemies, as the Pict's Wall, Offa's Ditch: and that in China, to compare things small to great. Their religion is at large described by Caesar. Their priests were Druids. Some of their temples I pretend to have restored, as Avebury, Stonehenge, etc. as also British sepulchres. Their waie of fighting is lively sett down by Caesar. Their camps with their way of meeting antagonists I have sett down in another place. They knew the use of iron. They were two or three degrees, I suppose, less savage than the Americans.'

In the course of these speculations Aubrey has made use of natural history (soils and woods), Classical writers (Caesar), folk-culture (coracles), field-work (hill-forts and linear earthworks) and comparative ethnology (American Indians). Prehistorians from the earliest days of their subject have relied to a

78

considerable extent on ethnology to provide models of early societies. In *Prehistoric Times*, published in 1865, Sir John Lubbock wrote: 'If we wish clearly to understand the antiquities of Europe, we must compare them with the rude implements and weapons still, or until lately, used by savage races in other parts of the world. In fact the Van Diemaner and South American are to the antiquary what the opossum and the sloth are to the geologist.'

Few anthropologists or archaeologists would now agree with General Pitt-Rivers that 'The existing races, in their respective stages of progression may be taken as the *bona fide* representatives of antiquity'. Contemporary 'primitive' societies are not stagnant or fossilized societies, and direct analogies between them and prehistoric groups can be dangerous. One has only to think of North America between the sixteenth and nineteenth centuries with its myriad of shifting Indian cultures. Almost no human groups are now

John White's illustrations (1585–90) of a North American Indian (*left*) and a Pict (*right*), both seen as romantic painted savages. The discovery of native peoples in America influenced the Old World's view of its own prehistoric ancestors.

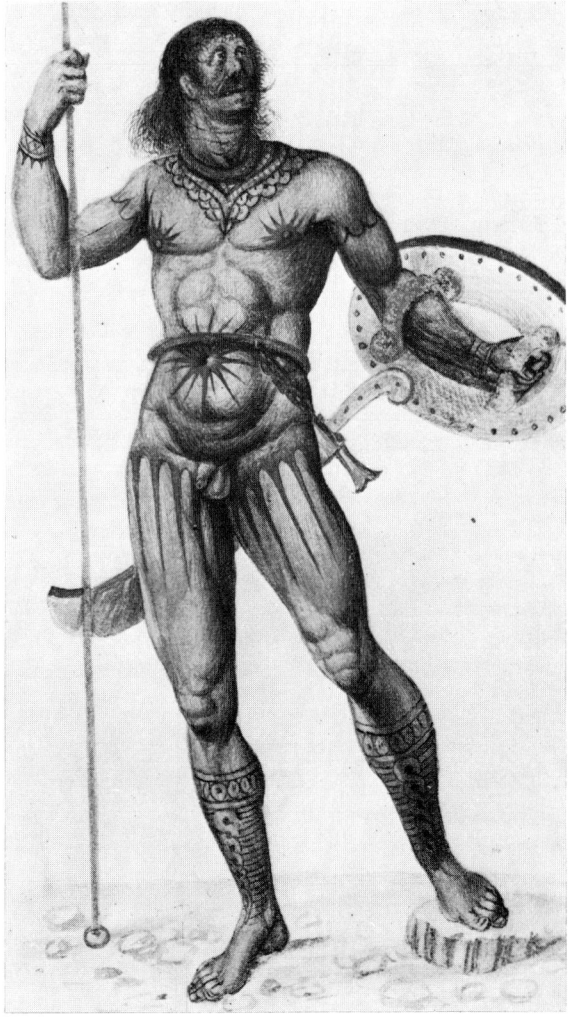

known which have not been affected in some way by contact with more technologically advanced cultures: the life of the Sioux changed dramatically with the arrival of the Spaniards' horses; equally drastic was the effect of European diseases such as measles; Australian Aborigines flake spear points from telegraph insulators and beer bottles; and the largely vegetarian diet of the !Kung bushmen may result from the destruction of the animal herds by Europeans. Human societies are a delicate balance of interacting factors which rarely stand still for long, and crude analogies may be misleading.

Ethnographers, ancient and modern, have been important in broadening our perspectives. Some of the most important accounts of 'primitive' societies are, themselves, centuries old—Herodotus describing the exotic burial rites of the Scythians, Caesar and Tacitus on the Britons and Germans, Ibn Fadlan in tenth-century Russia, Raleigh in South America, the Jesuit Jean de Brébeuf among the Huron, or Captain Cook in New Zealand. None of these people were objective, trained ethnographers but they all left important accounts of the people they had seen or heard about. We have to try to be aware of their personal interests and prejudices and treat their accounts like any other historical document.

Roman writers have bequeathed a substantial body of ethnographic information about the Celts, ranging from descriptions of storage pits, their crops and livestock to clothes, drinking habits, fondness for head-hunting, tattooing and the influence of the Druids. Archaeologists in their study of British prehistory also rely on analogies from more recent societies. At the Iron Age farm of Little Woodbury in Wiltshire Gerhard Bersu convincingly showed that the pits were not used as underground dwellings but for storage. Similar methods of preserving agricultural produce are known from Africa and North America. Groups of four and six post-holes were explained as above-ground granaries, which are still constructed in central Europe and India. More recently, Geoffrey Wainwright has pointed out the similarity between the large circular timber structures inside our henge monuments and the council-houses of the Creek Indians of Georgia. Colin Renfrew has examined the modern, megalithic tomb-builders of Madagascar in relation to British Neolithic communities and applied the anthropologist's concept of 'chiefdoms' to British prehistory.

Often the analogies used by archaeologists seem rather crude and arbitrary, and there are obvious dangers in comparing groups possibly 4,000 miles and years apart. It is surprising that so little interest has been shown in the study of British folk-culture, but the general feeling is that little has survived. The Industrial Revolution and the divorce from the land have probably resulted in a great loss of folk and oral tradition, more so than in Scandinavia, central or southern Europe. It is still, nevertheless, a neglected subject. The situation is rectified only by such stalwarts as author George Ewart Evans with his superb accounts of East Anglian tradition. Certainly, his writings on beliefs connected with horses (in, for example, *The Pattern under the Plough*, 1966)

Celtic horses: (*bottom*) from a British coin; (*top*) a vessel handle from Silchester. The beaked head of the former resembles that of the White Horse of Uffington.

80

provide fascinating insights for the student of the Iron Age beset by 'ritual burial of horse skulls' or images of horses on coins and cut into chalk downland.

At a more mundane level the technology of 'primitive' and not so primitive people can throw light on the archaeological record. Matt impressions found on the bases of pots were explained by the textile specialist Grace Crowfoot when she observed in Palestine a woman potter place an unfired, coil-built pot firmly on a mat: 'The mat was moved round when the potter wished to give attention to another aspect of the pot. In this movement of the mat, short and discontinuous as it is, one may see, fossilized, one of the early stages in the evolution of the wheel.' Archaeologists do not always have to find exotic craftsmen; blacksmiths, carpenters or silversmiths and jewellers working in Birmingham may provide useful information. The cross on the base of a fourth-century Romano-British pewter plate found at Appleford, Oxfordshire, is not of Christian significance: six arcs were drawn with a compass to locate the centre of the vessel so that it could be mounted on a lathe and polished.

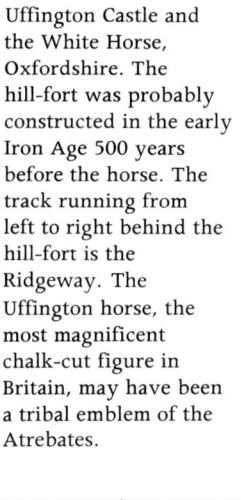

Uffington Castle and the White Horse, Oxfordshire. The hill-fort was probably constructed in the early Iron Age 500 years before the horse. The track running from left to right behind the hill-fort is the Ridgeway. The Uffington horse, the most magnificent chalk-cut figure in Britain, may have been a tribal emblem of the Atrebates.

In America anthropology has not been used simply to provide answers to specific questions; its influence has been more profound. The philosophy and fundamental aims of archaeology have been much in question in the late 60s and early 70s, and the debate spread to this side of the Atlantic. The arguments centred principally around the question of whether archaeology conformed to various definitions of a scientific subject and what archaeologists should aim to do. The details of these arguments are of interest only to students of archaeological metaphysics, but gradually the more sensible ideas are being put into practice.

Archaeology in the 70s is substantially different from the archaeology of twenty years ago. It has a battery of new techniques, many of which are listed in D. Brothwell and E. Higgs's *Science in Archaeology* (1964). Most important is the development of isotopic dating methods and the use of computers and statistical techniques. The latter have aroused passionate feelings among the largely arts-educated and innumerate British archaeological fraternity, but large-scale excavations and the necessity of dealing with vast quantities of data are resulting in a more common-sense and pragmatic attitude to these tools of the trade.

There is still a fundamental difference between those archaeologists, usually from a social-science background, who feel that 'lawlike generalization' should be the end-product of the subject and the doubters who, with Grahame Clark, believe that 'whereas the natural sciences deal with phenomena which conform to natural laws, archaeology is concerned with the results of human activities and with a multitude of unique events conditioned by cultural and even personal factors—in a word, with the phenomena of history'. They would claim that all too often the 'lawlike generalizations' are of extreme banality. Nevertheless, the appeal for a more rigorous analysis of archaeological method and theory is a valid one. Archaeology is gradually coming to realize that it is responsible for itself and must evolve its own principles and practices. It should not run along tracks laid by historians or anthropologists if it is to tackle seriously the questions posed by two million years or more of human existence. But the careful study of sites and societies where historical and anthropological evidence is also available will enable archaeologists to assess the limits of their evidence and test their theories.

6 The archaeologist at work

Five hundred years ago the Percys of Northumberland rode down into the hamlet of Hubberholme in the Yorkshire Dales, leaving the harassed deer of Langstrothdale Chase in peace while they imbibed spiritual and liquid refreshment. As the party clattered away from the isolated church and hostelry, scattering the flocks of Yockenthwaite and Deepdale, farms for 1,000 years, they might have wondered at a small circle of stones by the soft grassy banks of the beck. Five centuries later the sheep still graze the slopes of the dale, the moors are still a hunting-ground; grouse have replaced the deer, the Land-Rover the horse, and businessmen the feudal lords; but the land has changed little, and the circle of stones remains, as it has now for over 2,000 years. This prehistoric hut circle has avoided the flensing sweep of the plough, the deadly embrace of concrete or even conifers; it still exists, not because anyone has tried to protect it but because it never got in anyone's way.

About twenty kilometres due north of Langstrothdale the black-eyed ruin of Crackpot Hall stares down a rock and sheep-strewn valley, a scene of almost Alpine tranquillity. According to the Ordnance Survey map, a walk of three kilometres over the 600 m high moor to the east should bring us to the deserted dale of Gunnerside. Yet as the unwary hiker approaches, he sees a vision of hell: blasted hillsides, heaps of cinder, tunnels and stark, stone ruins. The heat has gone out of these leadmines, but the shock of their presence remains, an industrial monument on an epic scale. This then is the zone of preservation where changes occur but do not swamp the landscape, where sheep still graze over the hummocks of Celtic farmsteads and the mellowing scars of the Industrial Revolution.

It is possible for the observant dalesman to unravel the skeins of human activity from the visible traces that remain in the landscape. But what of the zone of destruction, the richer lowlands, the factory floor of one of Britain's most successful industries—farming, where 28,000 hectares are lost every year under roads, housing and quarries? Has the scouring gone so far that the past is irretrievably lost? In some places this is true, but the impact of ancient man has been considerable, and a vast amount of evidence remains.

The area around Barton Court Farm between Abingdon and Radley in Oxfordshire is a not untypical piece of lowland English landscape, though nowhere can be quite typical among such great variety and contrast. I cannot

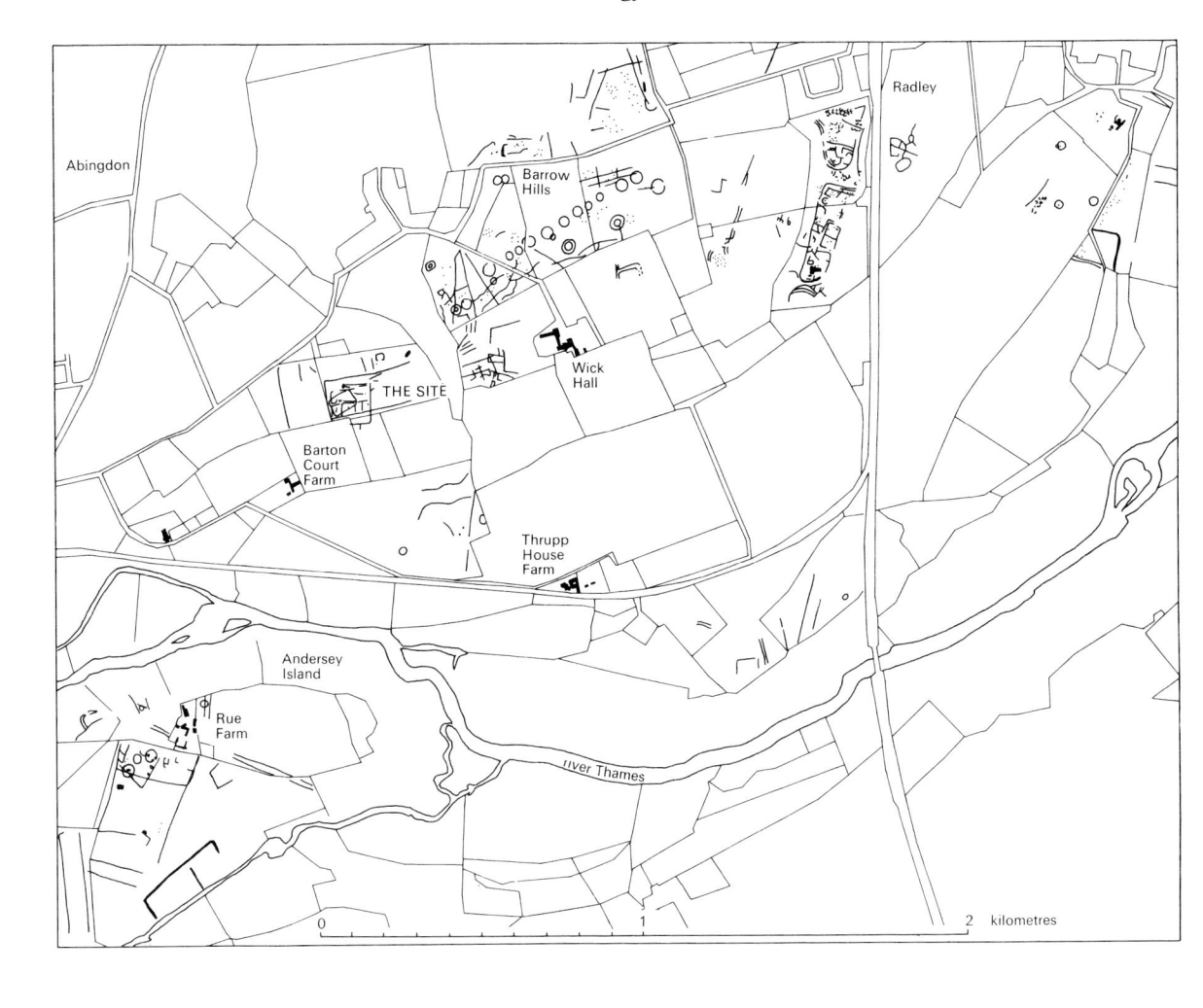

The area around
Barton Court Farm,
Abingdon, with crop
marks superimposed on
the modern landscape.

pretend this is just a spot chosen at random to show how the clever archaeologist can conjure up the past from thin air. I, and many other people, have
spent much of the past five years working over this particular piece of ground,
and for this reason it will serve to illustrate the archaeologists' methods and
the types of historical information that can be squeezed out of the countryside.

Maps

A careful study of the available maps is the first priority for any field-work
project. Modern Ordnance Survey maps at a variety of scales show the
present pattern of fields, farms, roads, villages, streams or rivers, hills and
valleys. The relevant geology map and soil map, if it is available, are also
essential. While solid geology changes very slowly, it is important to remember
that soils may have been modified since prehistoric times, very often by the
action of man himself. An idealized cross-section of the Thames Valley would

84

show the river in its flood plain with a series of steps on either side. These are the terraces of gravel deposited during the Ice Age by rivers flowing out of the Cotswolds and made up of millions of limestone pebbles. Barton Court Farm sits high and dry on the second of the gravel terraces, 7.5 m above the Thames.

We can begin to deepen our perspective by hunting out older maps. The first-edition Ordnance Survey maps will extend our view back to the early years of the nineteenth century, as will the maps accompanying the Tithe and Enclosure Awards. Michael Aston and Trevor Rowley describe the potential variety of maps available in their book *Landscape Archaeology* (1974). The local record office is the first place to look. Because of recent local government reorganization our area suffers from a split personality, and we have to search in the Reading and Oxford Offices as well as the Bodleian Library in Oxford. Looking through their indexes brings other maps to light, particularly John Rocque's *A Topographical Survey of the County of Berks, 1761.* His surveying was not as accurate as it might have been, but still the map contains a mine of

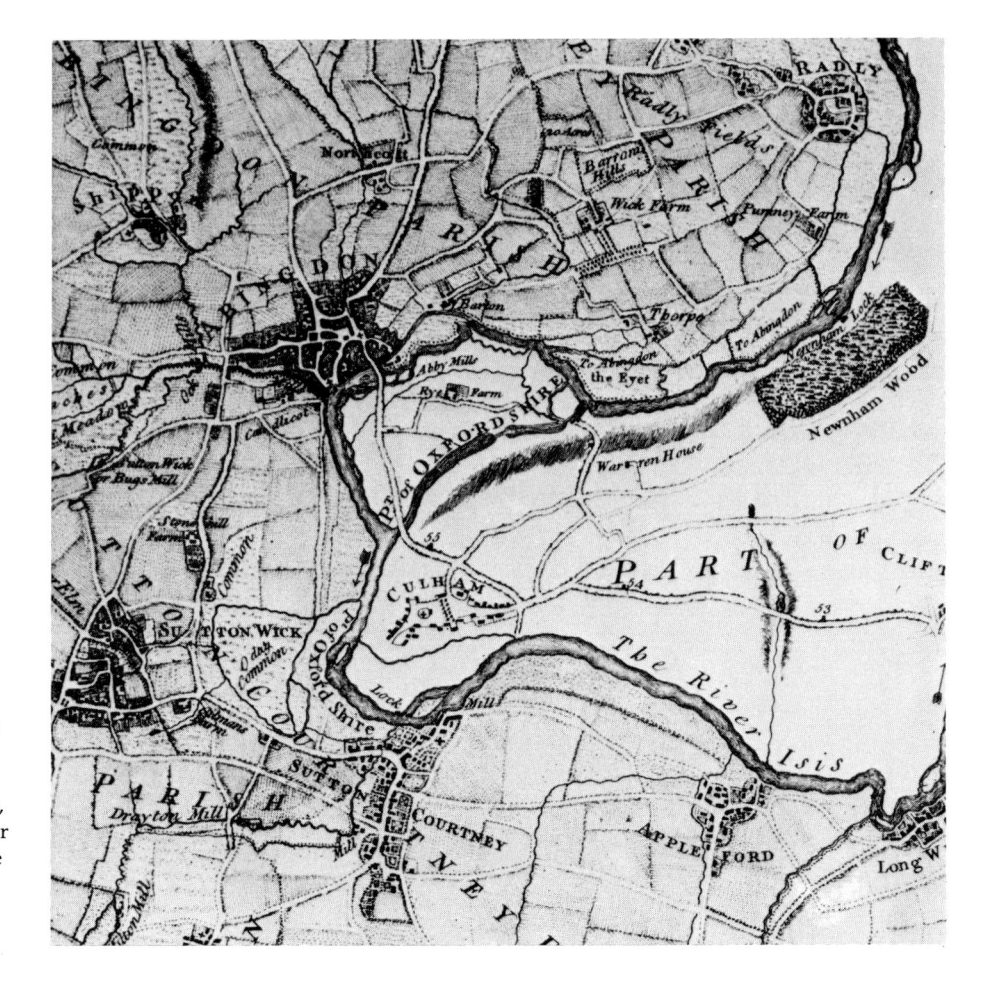

Maps, such as the one of the area around Barton Court Farm made by John Rocque, are an essential tool for the study of landscape history. (Compare it with the modern map on page 84.)

information about land use, the rough size and shape of fields and what farms, villages and roads were in existence 200 years ago. We can follow the cartographer even further, because in the local-authority offices in Abingdon there is an unexpected bonus, called the Monk's Map. Faded, crudely drawn and nearly 2 m long, this rather myopic, bird's-eye view of Abingdon was probably drawn in the early sixteenth century. It shows the layout of the town, the Thames, Barton Court, Thrupp Farm and a number of other farms and hamlets.

Place-names

One of the most interesting aspects of our maps is the great number of names they contain. Some of them are self-explanatory, like Gooseacre Farm, but Barton, Wick and Thrupp do not make much sense in modern English. Many villages, rivers and fields have names which seem meaningless today: this is simply because they were given many centuries ago by Old English speakers or even their Celtic predecessors. Fortunately, in this area much of the work of studying these names has been done by Dr Margaret Gelling in her mammoth, three-volume work *The Place-Names of Berkshire*. This is one of the county surveys issued by an admirable organization called the English Place-Name Society. So far twenty-six counties have been covered and another eight are in preparation. We are particularly lucky because Dr Gelling's book is the most recent and up-to-date in the whole series.

Barton Court Farm is one of the most significant names, because the whole of this area, including Abingdon, is called *Bertune* in the 'Domesday Book', William the Conqueror's great inventory of 1086. Originally, the name Barton meant, literally, 'a barley farm'. It came to refer, more specifically, to land belonging to an estate and used to produce its own food rather than being rented out to a tenant. The owners of this Barton in the eleventh century were the monks of Abingdon Abbey, and the vast areas of land which they held helped to make Abingdon one of the richest monasteries in the country. The name implies that barley-growing was important as early as the Saxon period, and this is supported by medieval records which tell of barley brought to the abbey for brewing.

The Barton land close by the river is suitable for grazing, and another name helps here. Thrupp Farm is near to the Thames, and although the land around it floods, the farm itself sits on a slightly higher patch of gravel, surrounded by huge drainage ditches. The main farmhouse is fairly modern, but nearby is a black and white half-timbered cottage, which suggests the farm may be of some age. The Old English name *thrupp* or *throp* simply means 'hamlet', and old maps reveal that it used to be a slightly larger place than it is now. The name first appears in a document of 1170, part of the chronicle of Abingdon Abbey, which says that Thrupp supplied the Abbey with eels and cheese.

The importance of cattle-grazing on the Thames-side meadow is reflected in another name—Wick Hall, *La Wyk* in 1284, which means dairy farm. So on

the evidence of place-names and various documents we can see that three of the farms in our area existed by the twelfth century, and probably earlier, forming part of Abingdon Abbey's estate; we can even get some idea of what they were producing.

The place-names can give us clues to an even older settlement: north of Wick Hall on Rocque's map is a field called Barrow Hills. There is only a flat arable field today, but it suggests that when the name was given there were burial mounds to be seen.

Aerial photographs

The gravel terraces of the Thames Valley are particularly favourable for the production of crop marks, so aerial photographs are an extremely important form of evidence. As part of the archaeological research project in the upper Thames Valley, all the crop marks appearing on thousands of oblique and vertical photographs were plotted on to maps.

These photographs seem to X-ray the landscape: the fields are covered with the graffiti of previous generations; circles, squares and lines appearing in the crops reveal traces of the buried past. But some of these marks are not man-made: Barrow Hills has a tracery of irregular lines running across it, cracks in the surface of the gravel caused by intense frost action during the Ice Age. Other marks are the superficial results of modern agriculture made by ploughing, and other, suspiciously straight lines are field drains.

Barrow Hills, Radley, Oxfordshire. In a traditionally arable area earthworks have long since been ploughed away, but the buried traces of the past appear with uncanny clarity as marks in a crop of barley. It is possible to see a Neolithic burial enclosure (the oblong double ditches) and the post-holes of a hut circle (upper right), Bronze Age barrows (running in a line from top left), Saxon sunken huts (the small, solid, rectangular marks scattered across the field) and a Romano-British or Saxon cemetery (a shoal of small marks, centre right). The cobweb of lines that criss-cross the field is due to frost-cracking in the last Ice Age and is of no archaeological interest.

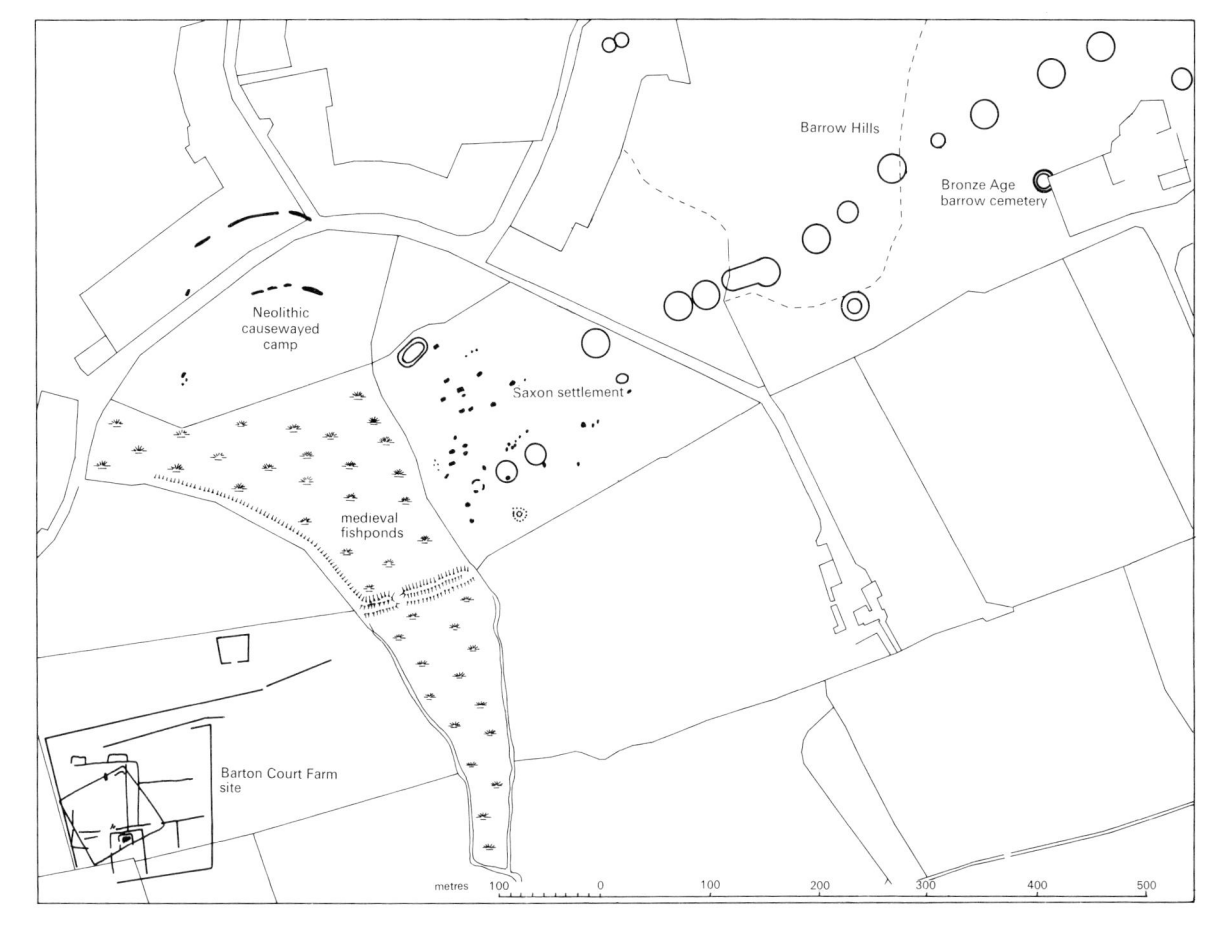

metres 100   0   100   200   300   400   500

Barton Court
Farm/Barrow Hills,
Oxfordshire: a plan of
the crop marks which
have appeared in the
study area, indicating
ancient settlements.

More conspicuously, in the yellowing barley of Barrow Hills Field is a series of large green circles, 30–40 m across. These are the remnants of what gave the field its name at least 400 years ago. The corn is tall and thick over the ditches which once surrounded the burial mounds themselves. The plough has removed the mounds but it cannot destroy the rings of silty soil with which the gravel terrace is veined. Barrows can date to various periods, but the linear arrangement suggests these are Bronze Age, second millennium BC, and, as we shall see, excavation has proved this to be the case.

The circles are only one element among many, and we must try to sort the crop marks into their relative sequence. At the very beginning of the history of settlement come the interrupted arcs of part of a Neolithic causewayed camp, severed now by Radley Road. We have discussed these important tribal centres in a previous chapter, and in recent years an increasing number have been discovered from the air. Immediately to the east is a double-ditched enclosure, rectangular in shape, with a spot in the centre. Exactly what this is must, without excavation, remain uncertain, but it may be a Neolithic burial site, the spot in the centre marking the position of a grave. More

88

difficult to see is a series of small marks forming three or four concentric rings near the south-eastern corner of this same field. These probably indicate the post-holes of a large timber structure, reminiscent of those excavated by Geoffrey Wainbright in the henges of Durrington and Marden (see page 40).

The field has a rash of small rectangular and oval marks on it. The larger, slightly rounded ones are the remains of sunken huts, with their floors dug into the ground, indicating that a substantial Saxon settlement, covering at least 4 hectares, once existed here. Smaller marks, not visible on the photographs printed here, are graves, most probably contemporary with the Saxon settlement.

Immediately to the south-west of these crop marks is a triangle of marshy land fed by streams which enclose the causewayed camp on two sides. The distinctive V-shape is cut across by a large earthwork near its narrow end. Now known as Daisy Banks, this great mound once acted as the dam for Abingdon Abbey's fishponds. A few hundred metres to the south-west another crop mark complex appears, a series of rectangles and squares overlying one another, probably of Iron Age and Romano-British date. The other major concentration of marks is alongside the railway line south of Radley, which probably indicates a large Romano-British village bounded by ditches.

Comparison with the soil map is very revealing, for all the crop marks of settlements lie on patches of the driest (so-called Sutton) soil, and the shape of the Radley settlement reflects exactly that of the patch of soil. Is this a case of early settlers showing their canniness and knowledge of soil types, or is the evidence biased because the areas of Sutton soils show crop marks better than anywhere else? Excavation and field-work suggest the former is true.

Archaeological records

An essential part of any research is to check the records that exist of previous work in an area. This entails looking through such obvious sources as the volumes of the *Victoria County History*, the Royal Commission for Historical Monuments volume, if you are lucky enough to be in an area that has been investigated (ours has not), the local archaeological journal and many other possible works. There are also archives to be searched, such as the Ordnance Survey files in Southampton, museums and, possibly, the county archaeological record.

This area differs from most in having attracted a number of archaeological excavators. Between 1927 and 1929 E. T. Leeds, Keeper of Antiquities at the Ashmolean Museum, reported on his work at the causewayed camp in the *Antiquaries' Journal*. He followed this by digging some of the Barrow Hills circles. In fact, between 1931 and 1945 various archaeologists put trenches through ten of them. Some of the finds were quite spectacular, including a fine pair of gold, basket-shaped earrings, and confirmed that the barrows belonged

to the Bronze Age. In 1945 Richard Atkinson of the Ashmolean Museum, later Professor of Archaeology at Cardiff University, discovered a Romano-British cemetery of the fourth century in Barrow Hills Field, and in 1963 further work on the causewayed camp also uncovered remains of Saxon sunken huts.

Half a dozen campaigns of excavation had taken place in the area of Barrow Hills up to 1963 but mostly on a very small scale, uncovering less than 2 per cent of the archaeological complex.

Land use and destruction

The diagram on page 88 shows the known sites, but many of them no longer exist. The land of the second gravel terrace, on which Barton Court Farm and Barrow Hills stand, is principally used as arable for growing barley and oil-seed rape. The action of the plough has continually planed off any man-made features presumptuous enough to stand above the surrounding level. In some places ploughing is actively cutting into the below-ground archaeological remains, threatening to remove the slight traces that survive.

This part of the county is subject to great social and economic pressures, and farming is being replaced by radically new forms of land use. In the 40s Barrow Hills lost seven of its circles to gravel extraction. Since then, another has been covered by houses, and in 1976 the ninth was destroyed by a new road. The causewayed camp has mostly disappeared under houses, and in 1972 the whole of Barton Court Farm was sold by Berkshire County Council for over £2 million for residential development. The farm buildings, which included a fine old barn, no longer exist; they were bulldozed away so as not to confuse the architects of the new estate.

On the lower ground of the first terrace a new landscape is being created by the drag lines of the gravel quarries. The whole area immediately north and south of the railway line that runs past Thrupp is being dug out, completely destroying any archaeological remains that exist there.

Field-work

Having researched the background to an area, there is no substitute for getting outdoors and becoming intimately acquainted with the countryside at first hand.

Most of the fields on our map have been examined at different times of year. Ideally, this should be done systematically, dividing the field into units of an appropriate size and walking over them at a steady pace, recording the position of finds on a plan. There are very few earthworks in this area, save for the banks of the fishponds and ridge and furrow under the turf of the paddocks by Wick Hall. All the other fields are arable, so the best time to walk over them is after they have been ploughed, in decent light but preferably with little or no shadow. It is often possible to get some idea of the date of a

crop-mark complex from the pottery sherds scattered over its surface. The Barton Court Farm site was littered with hundreds of fragments of Romano-British pottery, looking like so many bits of plant pot to the uninitiated but really quite easy to identify as belonging to the third and fourth centuries AD. Also, fragments of white plaster and cubes of limestone indicated that there were the remains of a substantial Roman building below the ground. A plan of the pot scatter can reveal the focus of settlement and may also suggest which areas were cultivated. Bits of pottery often found their way into the muck heap of the ancient farm and were carried out with the manure to be spread on the fields. A thin scatter of abraded sherds may indicate the extent of a settlement's fields or the infields which were regularly fertilized.

It is important to remember that some kinds of pottery are more durable than others. The hard Romano-British wares seem to be almost indestructible, but prehistoric and Saxon pottery, fired at lower temperatures, is softer and more friable, tending to break up in the ploughsoil. When a site at Ashville, on the west side of Abingdon, was examined, it produced masses of Romano-British pottery and little else. Yet when it was subsequently excavated, only three Romano-British features were found among dozens of Iron Age pits and hut circles.

Worked flint is often a more reliable indicator of prehistoric activity than pottery. The fields around Thrupp have been carefully explored and produced many Neolithic and Bronze Age arrowheads. Until recently the ground immediately adjacent was marshy and alive with wildfowl, so these arrowheads seem to be the prehistoric equivalent of the cartridge cases that litter the ground nowadays.

There is one technique of the field-worker that we have had little opportunity to practise here and that is hedge dating. There are relatively few hedges in our piece of countryside, and most of them are nineteenth-century quickset hedges made up of hawthorn. More interesting, though, is the one along Barton Lane, the track leading to Thrupp. This occurs on the earliest maps, and although the hedge has been grubbed out along most of its length, the stretch which survives is unusually rich. The procedure for hedge dating is to count the species of perennial shrubs and trees in a section of hedge 27 m long. The ideal formula is that there is one species present for every century that the hedge has existed. There are too many problems for the results to be automatically accepted, but the Barton Lane hedge contains ten species, suggesting that it is 1,000 years old, and this is not unlikely considering the known history of Thrupp.

Excavation

Excavation ought to be the last resort of the archaeologist. Digging necessitates destruction and therefore should not be undertaken lightly. In 1974 the Oxfordshire Archaeological Unit produced a survey of the upper Thames

Valley, cataloguing all the known sites and making recommendations for preservation and excavation. The Barton Court Farm/Barrow Hills area was highlighted as under severe threat of destruction, while containing an important of prehistoric, Roman, Saxon and medieval sites. More important, it presented the opportunity to examine the history of a complete slice of landscape crossing some of the different ecological belts of the Thames Valley.

The phrase 'rescue archaeology' covers a multitude of sins from a careful, large-scale and costly dig, well in advance of a proposed development, to a frantic scramble in front of a juggernaut bulldozer. In a large area like this, given limited funds, it was necessary to work out a strategy whereby the maximum amount of information could be obtained within the available budget. A close watch was kept on the gravel pits around Thrupp, with the help of the local archaeological society, in order to salvage as much as possible as cheaply as possible. In contrast, a systematic excavation was mounted at Barton Court Farm on a settlement of many periods.

At Barton Court Farm the archaeological levels lie very close to the surface. The ploughsoil, about 30 cm deep, was peeled off, first by hand to get the feel of the site and then using a JCB mechanical digger. This revealed the bare, yellow surface of the gravel, pock-marked and criss-crossed with veins of dark, humic soil like a well-used sheet of blotting-paper. These were the pits, ditches and post-holes of multiple phases of occupation. Sections of these features were carefully removed in order to work out their relative age, to find material which would date them and, hopefully, to assess their function. One strip of the site had better preservation, where continual ploughing has piled up a bank or lynchet against a field boundary. Under this protective mantle the foundations of a Roman building survived, while elsewhere they had been planed off by the plough.

The excavation was a slow process, for the surface of the gravel had to be carefully cleaned over, particularly if the slight traces of timber buildings were to be found. Everything had to be planned and photographed, and the finds carefully washed and sent to the conservation laboratory for treatment. Many features were sampled for biological material—carbonized and water-logged plant remains, beetles, snail shells and animal bones. The excavation team was made up of a relatively small number of professional archaeologists— a draughtsman, finds assistant, zoologist and botanist—with assistance from a large number of volunteers from archaeological societies, local schools, British and foreign universities.

A brief summary of the principal phases may provide an idea of the complexity of the site.

Neolithic

A scatter of small pits across the site indicated that there was occupation in the third millennium BC. They contained carbonized grain, animal bones,

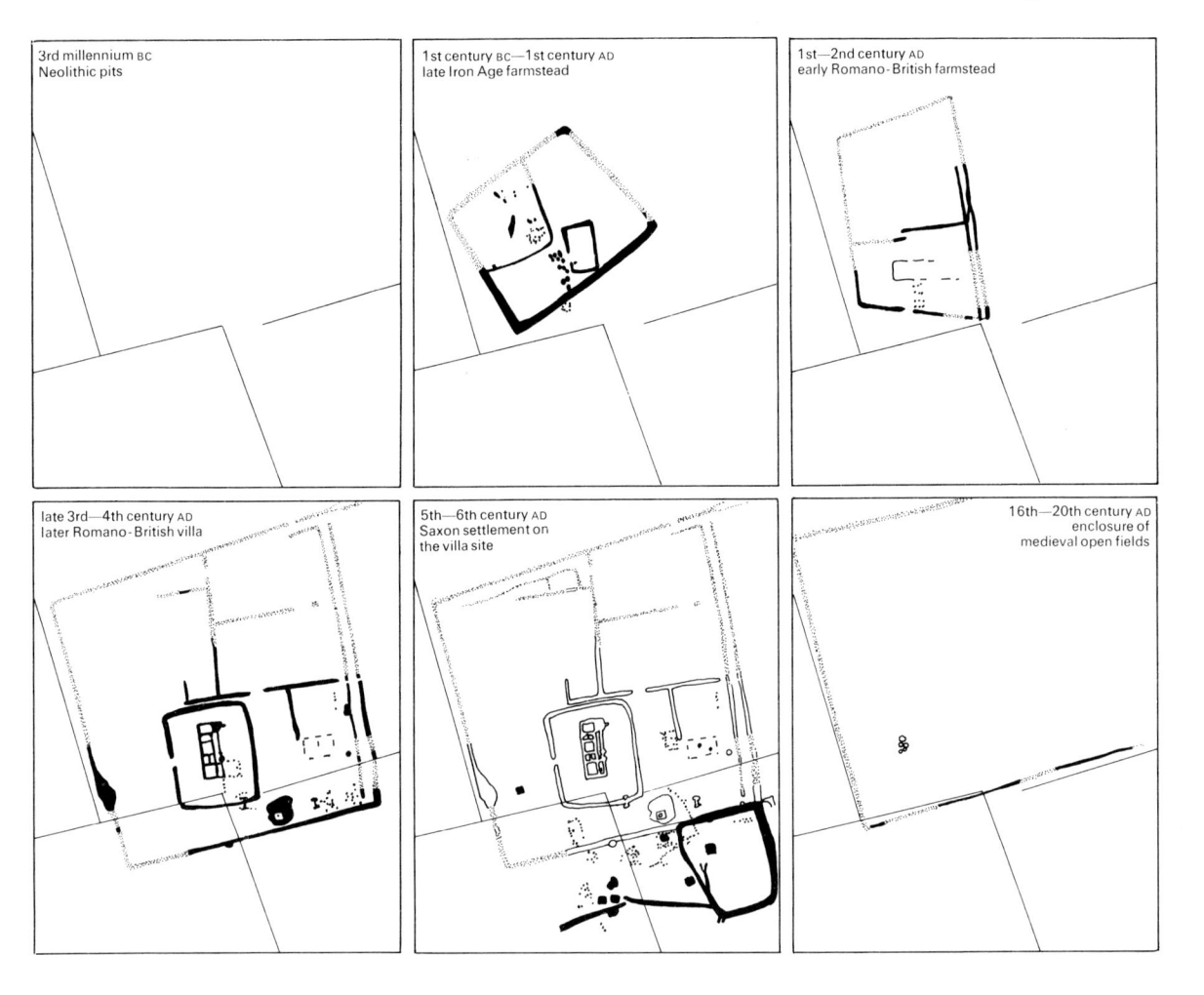

3rd millennium BC
Neolithic pits

1st century BC—1st century AD
late Iron Age farmstead

1st—2nd century AD
early Romano-British farmstead

late 3rd—4th century AD
later Romano-British villa

5th—6th century AD
Saxon settlement on
the villa site

16th—20th century AD
enclosure of
medieval open fields

Barton Court Farm: the phases of settlement at the site based on excavation evidence. The black lines represent those features which were excavated; stippled lines are features plotted from aerial photographs.

crude pottery and flint, and in one was the antler of a red deer. There were no traces of any structures, but house foundations need not have penetrated the gravel. The pottery appears to belong to a slightly later period than that of the causewayed camp, and preliminary uncalibrated radiocarbon dates from bone samples processed in the Harwell laboratory suggest a date of about 2000 BC.

Iron Age

After the Neolithic period, there was no evidence of occupation on this particular site until the first century BC. Then a farmstead appeared inside a ditched enclosure 75 m square. The ditch, 2 m wide and the same in depth, would not have been intended for defence in the military sense. It demarcated the settlement, kept domestic animals in and unwelcome ones out, and perhaps discouraged the would-be participants in the favourite Celtic sport of cattle rustling.

Above Barton Court Farm, Abingdon, Oxfordshire: the post-holes (centre) of a late Iron Age circular house and behind a large storage pit. They sit inside a ditched enclosure.

Above right The robbed-out remains of the late Romano-British farmhouse. Constructed at the end of the 3rd century AD, the house was systematically demolished in the 5th century and the stone carted away. Only the foundations in the bottom left-hand corner survive to any great extent.

Inside the main enclosure was a smaller, subsidiary one, containing a round house. Only the post-holes remained of what was, originally, a thatched hut with wattle and daub walls. Nearby was a large pit, one of those underground breadbins that the Celts were so fond of. It contained an archaeological bonus, a thick layer of black, carbonized grain. There were a dozen or so further storage pits in a cluster inside the main enclosure, but none of them held such a rich harvest of seeds.

Early Romano-British

The Iron Age farmstead was replaced by another, remarkably similar, arrangement shortly after the Roman Conquest of AD 43. Its pottery was mostly identical to that of the Iron Age settlement, but, gradually, better-fired, grey wares began to appear and some imported Continental vessels. This was still very much a Celtic farmstead, possibly even occupied by the descendants of the previous one, but with the merest gloss of Roman provincialism. The main house was no longer circular but instead a long, rectangular structure with plastered walls. A few Roman coins circulated, although a British one of Cunobelinus was also found. Roman pots, amphorae, *mortaria* and glossy red Samian tableware were the main indicators of the changing life-style.

Later Romano-British

By the late third century the Roman way of life was well established, and a new, substantial farmhouse was built. The building did not look very impressive during excavation because it had been literally taken to bits in the fifth century. The stone for the farmhouse, Coral Rag, was brought from quarries some four miles away. There is no stone on the gravel terraces, so if a building is abandoned, someone will soon remove it stone by stone. This does not make life easy for the archaeologist. Here, the building had been systematically demolished and even its foundations dug out, leaving what, in the digger's argot, are called *robber trenches*. These faint bands of discoloured soil were carefully traced and excavated, leaving a negative impression of the building in the ground.

94

A model of the small Romano-British villa at Barton Court Farm, Abingdon, Oxfordshire, made by Mr Ron James of the Oxfordshire County Museum at Woodstock.

The farmhouse, originally, must have been quite substantial with six rooms on the ground floor, a corridor, a cellar and probably an upper storey. The walls were plastered and painted in rather predictable bands of red and green, reminiscent of an old-fashioned railway waiting-room. The floors had been tessellated with small limestone cubes before the plough carved them up. The windows were glazed, and the house roofed in Cotswold stone slates and red ceramic tiles and sealed with lead. The great advantage of this type of house over the circular Iron Age ones was the element of privacy made possible by the existence of the corridor. It was not equipped with that other civilized domestic luxury of the Roman world, the underfloor heating system: these hardy Romano-Britons must have relied on braziers.

Many Roman villas have been excavated, but there has been a tendency to concentrate on the house and its architecture to the detriment of the business side of what was, after all, an agricultural estate. The villa was not just a self-sufficient farm; it aimed to provide agricultural produce for sale in a cash economy. One of the archaeological aims was to find out how this estate used its land and what it produced. For this reason the excavation was extended to the chequer-board of paddocks and enclosures which surrounded the farm-house. Evidently, several of them were used to pen animals. In one enclosure a couple of sheep skeletons lay in the ditches. In addition there was a water-hole, its sides trampled down by the hooves of thirsty animals, and nearby there were two pairs of sheep-shears. Cereal growing was also important, for in the centre of another paddock there was a corn-drying oven. This stone, T-shaped structure sunken into the ground would have had a table-like top, heated from below by a small fire. In order to prevent it sprouting and rotting during storage grain was dried on this large-scale hotplate. Fortunately, some of the grains trickled into the flue and were carbonized by the heat of the fire. In the prehistoric period water had to be fetched from a spring a few minutes' walk from the site. The Romano-Britons had two wells in the yards: one, 4.8 m deep and lined with stone, had 3.6 m of water in it besides thirteen leather

sandals, a bucket, several complete pots, a spear and many pieces of ironwork.

Another area of the Roman farm had a less prosaic purpose: it was used as a burial ground for the tiny corpses of about forty new-born children. The main cemetery for the adult occupants of the farm was probably that excavated by Professor Atkinson at Barrow Hills. In communities with a high infant mortality rate the unfortunate ones are commonly disposed of unceremoniously around the settlement, in ditches or shallow graves, and are not taken to the adult burial ground. Only two skeletons here had grave goods: these slightly older children were accompanied by the skulls of a dog and a sheep.

Saxon

Saxon urn with large bosses and pedestal base.

One of the most interesting episodes in the study of the changing settlement at Barton Court Farm is the period in the fifth century when the Romano-British occupants were replaced by Germanic ones. The division between Roman Britain and Saxon England used to be seen as clear-cut and catastrophic: Britons running like lemmings into the western seas pursued by fire and sword, while Saxons took over a deserted and generally forested countryside. Of course, this clichéd image is largely fictitious. Mention has already been made of the evidence for a phase of controlled Saxon settlement in and around the Romano-British towns like Dorchester and Canterbury, when mercenaries were introduced by the Roman and, later, British authorities. Several attempts have been made, not entirely successfully, to show that Saxons took over villa estates and perpetuated them. All that we can say at this stage is that the evidence points in this direction but is not conclusive. At Barton Court Farm the Romano-British way of life certainly seems to come to a gradual rather than a dramatic stop. The local pottery industry no longer functions; newly minted coins do not arrive after the 390s AD; and the farmhouse is systematically demolished.

There is a certain amount of evidence that Saxon farmers followed the British almost immediately and may have even overlapped with them. In the smaller Roman building, which may have been used as a smithy, a very interesting hoard of coins was found. All were from the last issues to arrive in Britain just before AD 400, but their worn condition suggests they were probably in use until about AD 430. In the middle of the same building were two burials, both Saxon women, pathetically cradling new-born infants, who had presumably died in childbirth. A gaudy, gilded bronze brooch suggests the burials occurred in the sixth century.

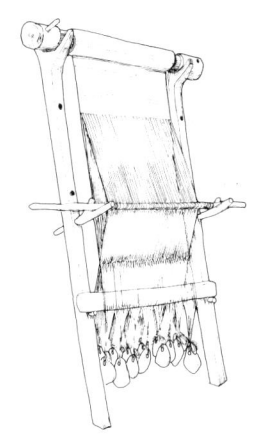

Reconstruction of a Saxon warp-weighted loom.

Elsewhere on the site sherds of soft, black pottery, speckled with fragments of chaff, appeared. This so-called 'grass-tempered pottery', made from clay mixed with straw and manure and often decorated with stamped rosettes, was the most common clue to the arrival of the new settlers. The fact that much of it occurred in the ditches of the villa enclosures suggested that there was no great gap between the old and new occupants.

The Saxons not only buried their dead and their rubbish on the site; they

also built houses and farmed the land. Faint traces survived of the post-holes of rectangular timber buildings, but more easy to locate were the pits, 3–4 m square, of sunken huts. All of them produced evidence of textile manufacture, including bone tools and spindle whorls, and one of them had a line of lead loom weights lying on its floor. These were hung on the warp, or vertical threads, of an upright loom to hold it taut.

The Saxon material dated to the fifth and sixth centuries and possibly a little later. At some time in the late sixth or seventh century the site was abandoned as a settlement. There is complicated historical evidence to suggest that around AD 670 the monastic community of Abingdon was granted the land hereabouts by the royal house of Wessex. If this is so, then it might explain why the small community here, and possibly the larger one across the field at Barrow Hills, moved off the site in a reorganization of an estate which may have existed since Iron Age times.

Medieval and later

Only the traces of strip fields etched into the gravel surface indicate that for nine centuries this land was cultivated on behalf of Abingdon Abbey. By the fourteenth century the national economic situation was in a state of flux, there was a labour shortage, and large demesne farms were an anachronism. Parts of Barton were rented out in 1536 to a certain John Audlett, the Abbot's bailiff and steward. Abingdon Abbey, one of the richest in the country, was not noted for its piety, and Piers Plowman predicted its downfall:

> *And thanne shal the abbot of Abyndoun*
> *and all his issu for evere*
> *Have a knokke of a kynge*
> *and incurable the wound.*

In 1538 Henry VIII delivered the 'knokke'. With the dissolution of the Abbey, John Audlett, and later his wife's family, retained Barton and they may have been responsible for enclosing part of the open fields. One of the latest features on the excavation was a shallow ditch, visible on the aerial photographs, apparently put round a parcel of strips. A coin of Henry VIII appropriately indicated the date of its digging.

Post-excavation

Once an excavation is completed, members of the archaeological team are faced with the even greater task of analysing their records and the material which they have found. A year later the work on the Barton Court Farm evidence is nearing completion, and a mass of data is issuing from the specialists who have studied the building material, tools, coins, textile equipment, millstones, ornaments, pottery, human and animal bones, botanical remains and many other types of material.

A silver coin of the Roman emperor Valens (AD 374–8) from Barton Court Farm, one of the many different types of evidence which help to date the features of an excavation. The letters at the bottom of the coin, TRPS, show that it was minted in Trier.

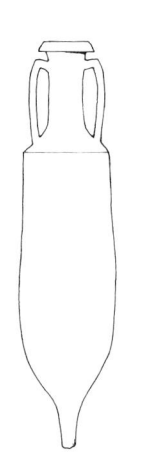

Roman amphora of a type found at Barton Court Farm—the tin cans of the ancient world in which Mediterranean products such as wine, oil, fish, sauce, dried fruit and grain were packed.

Mortarium of the late 1st century AD stamped with the potter's name SOLLUS.

Pottery

Almost 2 tonnes of pottery were found on the site and over 100,000 sherds. All of it was classified on the basis of its fabric (i.e. the clay, minerals in it and the method of manufacture), and a catalogue of vessel forms was compiled into which every identifiable sherd was incorporated. Pottery is useful for dating the features in which it is found, but there are many other kinds of information that it can provide. Pots can reveal trading patterns by their place of origin and their quantity. Their function is important: were they used for storage of goods, cooking or as tableware? Were they cheap or expensive?

From the Romano-British settlement the pottery acts as an indicator of the level of Romanization. Although most of the vessels were native types, fragments of amphorae appeared in the late first century AD. These were the tin cans and barrels of the Roman world, used to transport oil, wine or even a rather unappetizing-sounding fish sauce. The minerals in the clay of our amphorae indicated that they came from Spain and southern Italy. The way to a Briton's loyalty may well have been through his stomach, and about this time *mortaria*, or grinding bowls which were useful for making purées, appear on the site. The finest one is stamped with the name of the potter, Sollus, who operated near St Albans at the end of the first century AD. By the fourth century Romano-British pottery was being manufactured in large-scale production centres. By comparing the percentages of vessels from the different centres we can see their relative importance in this part of the world. Although pottery is a relatively cheap and humble product, it may act as a social indicator. As the Roman farm became more prosperous, it bought in a greater number of tablewares, including red-painted bowls and platters, pointing to a greater degree of sophistication on the part of the occupants.

Biological remains

The study of plants and animals in relation to ancient man is a relatively new and important subject in which archaeologists are very much feeling their way.

The earliest evidence of agriculture in our area is from the causewayed camp and takes the form of grain impressions in pottery. When the pots were in the process of being manufactured and still soft, they were set down on the ground. Cereal grains littering the floor left their marks in the clay to be fossilized by the subsequent firing. These impressions would not be so relevant if the pots in which they were contained had been manufactured elsewhere. For this reason thin sections were taken from the vessels in order to analyse the clay and discover its source. No positively diagnostic minerals were present, but the pots probably originated locally, in which case so did the grains of emmer wheat and six-row barley contained in them.

Samples of charcoal from the same site suggest that in the fourth millennium BC the gravel terraces were extensively cleared. These include hawthorn,

Fat hen (*Chenopodium album*), an edible weed whose seeds occur in Iron Age and Roman grain deposits at Barton Court Farm.

old man's beard (*Clematis vitalba*), ivy, blackthorn, wild privet and apple which nowadays occur most often in hedges and do not suggest a densely wooded landscape.

At Barton Court Farm some of the most interesting results have come from the analysis of carbonized plant remains found in storage pits and ovens. These consist principally of grain and the weed species harvested with the crop in which they grew. It could be argued that some of the weeds were included deliberately. Fat hen (*Chenopodium album*) occurs in the Iron Age storage pits (and for that matter in the stomachs of Iron Age bodies from Danish bogs), and although we know it nowadays as a weed of disturbed ground, it was cultivated and eaten in many countries until relatively recently. On the other hand, corn-cockle (*Agrostemma githago*) is anything but desirable, as any farmer without resort to herbicides knows: 'What hurt it doth among corne, the spoil unto bread, as well in colour, taste, and unholsomnes, is better known than desired.' We can add to this sixteenth-century condemnation that eating corn-cockle causes gastroenteritis in humans and can even kill animals.

Other weeds grow in certain types of soil and suggest which ground around the farm was cultivated. During the prehistoric periods it seems likely that the cornfields were on the dry second terrace. By the fourth century AD seeds of plants such as common spike-rush (*Eleocharis palustris*) indicate that the wet lands by the river were being cultivated. Salvage excavation provided likely confirmation when Roman ditches were found around Thrupp Farm. From the plant remains we can begin to reconstruct part of the economy of the successive farms, estimate the size of their estates, and analyse the changes that took place.

Finally, a word about animal bones, over 10,000 of which were collected at Barton Court Farm. Mixed farming seems to be the general rule from the earliest times, and wild animals play remarkably little part in the farmers' economy. Less than 1 per cent of the bones at the causewayed camp were deer's, but 85 per cent came from cattle. Cattle in fact predominate right through until the end of the Roman period. The fact that the cattle bones at the villa tend to be from bigger, older animals probably indicates that more of them were being used to pull carts and ploughs.

In the early Saxon period the impression is that the standard of farming deteriorated. Hunting and fishing became more important with bones of wild fowl, deer, pike, eel, perch and roach all on the increase. The number of horses was drastically reduced, but sheep and pigs increased—the last requiring woodland to root in.

At the time of writing this work is still continuing on the material from the sites in the Abingdon/Radley area, and further field-work and excavation are planned. We have only skimmed the surface but, hopefully, shown the type of information which can be gained from a piece of landscape in the front line of the destruction zone.

7 Archaeology in action

Archaeology attracts people for many reasons: it involves team-work; it appeals to those who like to combine physical outdoor activity with more academic study; and there is a strong element of occasional excitement and sense of discovery, even if preceded by hours of painstaking and unglamorous effort. Archaeology has, for many people, a sense of immediacy which is perhaps lacking in conventional documentary history. Students of archaeology usually deal with the primary evidence at first hand, and even the most blasé get a kick out of such direct contact with the past.

In some countries archaeology is very much the preserve of the erudite professional, and the general public is relegated to the role of spectator. Britain, in contrast, has a healthy tradition of amateur involvement, so that almost everyone is reasonably close to some form of archaeological organization. It is important to emphasize that the enthusiastic but unskilled can do a lot of damage if he or she takes this as an invitation to grab the garden spade and attack the nearest, defenceless archaeological site. The amateur, in the real sense of the word, can make a genuine and valuable contribution but only if he approaches the subject responsibly. Archaeology is not about finding curios for the mantelpiece.

So how does the enthusiastic reader get involved? Probably by joining a local archaeological society, an excavation or an evening class. It is impossible to say how many local archaeological and historical societies exist in this country. In my own county of Oxfordshire there are at least two dozen, varying from the long-established county society to small groups in the villages. Throughout the country in the past ten years there has been a great explosion in the number of amateur organizations. The Council for British Archaeology (CBA), which brings together the wide range of bodies involved in the national scene, has over 400 institutional members. The CBA can provide information about societies in England and Wales, but the local museum is often the best place to find out about the smaller groups which are springing up all the time.

These societies vary enormously in their character and activities. Some simply have lecture programmes throughout the winter months and excursions to sites, while others are actively involved in original and useful work. Amateur archaeologists can become familiar with their own neighbourhood

and their own neighbours in a way which is impossible for the professional who has to cover a wider area. Britain, as we have seen, has been occupied for many thousands of years, and vast numbers of ancient sites still await discovery. In recent years the emphasis has been on field-work, the systematic exploration of an area to locate as many archaeological sites of all periods as possible.

It might seem common sense that in a small, densely populated and intensively cultivated island we must know the whereabouts of most ancient sites. In fact, this is just not so. Not many months ago I accompanied a small group of field-workers along the valley of a small brook in Oxfordshire's Vale of White Horse. A mile up the valley we came across a solid line of rubble running across a ploughed field. Mixed in among the stones were fragments of Roman pottery, including the glossy red sherds of Samian ware, indicating that the original wall probably dated to the second century after Christ. A few hundred metres farther along we found distinct mounds of stone forming the outline of a large building. There were large dressed blocks, again masses of Roman pottery and an amber bead from a Saxon necklace. Subsequently, another Roman farmstead appeared on the opposite bank of the brook. A sortie by aeroplane produced crop marks of ditched enclosures, and examination of archaeological records showed that a large hoard of Roman coins had been found nearby many years ago. The whole of this shallow valley, in a populous part of southern England, is littered with the remains of Romano-British farms. There are two reasons why they had not been found before: the land was common meadow from at least the time of the 'Domesday Book' (1086) until the nineteenth century and had only recently been ploughed up to reveal the Roman rubble on the surface; secondly, it needed someone with an eye for the historic landscape to walk up a valley that led nowhere in particular.

A parish survey scheme has been pioneered in Cornwall and has resulted in a colossal increase in the number of known sites. In this type of effort an individual or a small group selects a single parish. The local maps, aerial photographs and documentary evidence are studied, every field in the parish is carefully walked over, usually several times, buildings are examined and everything from Stone Age axes to nineteenth-century milestones recorded. In such a scheme jobs can be found for everyone: the most hardy will tramp the ploughed fields, their eyes straining for tell-tale flint or pot sherds; others may prefer to analyse and draw the material that has been found and catalogue it for the local museum, study the documents and maps, or produce the group's newsletter. The successful Cornish formula has been adopted in many other counties and has helped to revolutionize our ideas about the density of population in the British Isles in the past. Particularly useful has been the way in which the best parish surveys have involved many non-archaeological groups and made people aware of their historic environment. As part of the Oxfordshire scheme Women's Institutes are collecting the

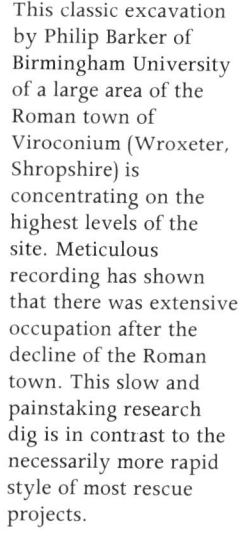

This classic excavation by Philip Barker of Birmingham University of a large area of the Roman town of Viroconium (Wroxeter, Shropshire) is concentrating on the highest levels of the site. Meticulous recording has shown that there was extensive occupation after the decline of the Roman town. This slow and painstaking research dig is in contrast to the necessarily more rapid style of most rescue projects.

Hibaldstow, South Humberside: rescue excavation of a Roman settlement alongside Ermine Street, about 30 km north of Lincoln. This large area excavation was photographed from the bucket of a crane about 25 m above the ground.

names of every field in their parishes; elsewhere schools, farmers, natural historical societies, teacher-training colleges and many others have become involved. And, of course, some of the most useful work is done by the dedicated and versatile loners who prefer to tackle the many strands of evidence in their own parish by themselves.

Sometimes field-work is geared towards particular subjects or problems. We may wish to know, for example, the number and variety of Romano-British settlements in a particular region or the extent of medieval woodland. In Northamptonshire three amateur archaeologists have in the past few years done a superb job of reconstructing the pattern of medieval open fields over a large part of the county.

102

The information that is recovered in field-walking should be precisely recorded and logged in a permanent record, usually to be found in the local museum. A site can neither be actively protected nor excavated unless its existence is known, and every dot on an archaeological distribution map adds to our knowledge of the past.

Most people assume that archaeology is about digging. Excavations can be exciting, they are newsworthy and they appeal to the imagination; they are also expensive, hard work and, in a sense, destructive. When archaeologists excavate a site they systematically take it to pieces. The evidence *in situ* usually has to be destroyed in order to be understood. The supply of archaeological sites is not infinite, so a dig should not be carried out unless there is a very good reason. As we have seen, in the past too much work was done irresponsibly and carelessly in the search for loot. Today, the spirit of conservation is more widespread, though many would say not widespread enough. To a certain extent this has inhibited research excavation. The stock of well-preserved and unthreatened sites is so relatively small that many archaeologists feel we should leave them alone for future generations with more advanced techniques of investigation. In recent years rescue excavations have become almost the general rule. This means that most sites are dug prior to their destruction by new housing, road-works, quarries or the many other manifestations of modern development.

The image of the rescue excavator as the intrepid, if harassed, kamikaze front line of the archaeological world, grasping the delicate evidence of the past from the maw of a voracious bulldozer, is now somewhat outdated. This type of salvage work is still necessary, but in many cases excavations are mounted on threatened sites well in advance of development. The most enlightened local authorities now make provision for excavation in their planning consents, and in some cases the work is financed by the developer himself. This is not to say that the situation regarding preservation or excavation is entirely satisfactory. Vast numbers of sites are destroyed without any investigation whatsoever. Coalmining, road-building, the spread of suburbia, stone and gravel quarrying, afforestation and ploughing unfortunately remove thousands of hectares of ancient landscape every year, and the majority without examination by archaeologists. Since the production of *Rescue Archaeology* in 1976, edited by Philip Rahtz, some of the heat has gone out of the 'Great Destruction Debate'. We should not become complacent about the loss of both our heritage and our evidence, but archaeologists need to state their priorities clearly and ensure that, while some loss is inevitable, adequate samples are both preserved and excavated.

Without the presence of the keen amateur hundreds of sites would have disappeared unrecorded and often unknown. But excavation is a skilled business, and it is best to learn the trade alongside experienced practitioners. It is not the aim of this short book to provide a guide to digging—several of these already exist. Most notable is *Techniques of Excavation* by Philip Barker,

the master of the meticulous techniques currently in use on the post-Roman layers of Wroxeter. The older stand-by, *Practical Archaeology*, by Barker's colleague at Birmingham University, Graham Webster, is a valuable introduction for all new and many not-so-new diggers. In the final analysis excavation skills cannot be learnt from a book; practice and example will be of far greater use.

The popular image of the patient archaeologist poised with trowel or paintbrush over some delicate find like a praying mantis is of limited truth. More often the work can be strenuous and more akin to navvying, but there is also the need for surveyors, draughtsmen, photographers and people to wash, mark, conserve and draw finds. Almost every subject is grist to the archaeologist's mill: a knowledge of geology, soil science, botany, zoology, statistics and all aspects of technology will stand the excavator, a jack of all trades, in good stead.

The basic skills are taught at a number of training excavations. Several extra-mural departments, including those at the universities of Birmingham, Bristol, Oxford and Cambridge, regularly organize such projects. Twenty or thirty people, ranging from absolute beginners to experienced enthusiasts, are usually involved. In the course of a week or a fortnight the students are introduced to digging, drawing, photography and the study of finds. For many people this is the ideal way to start in archaeology, though like all 'classroom situations' the training excavation does not always bear much resemblance to the real thing. Information about digs can best be found in the CBA's monthly *Calendar of Excavations*. This lists forthcoming training, rescue and research projects and the number of volunteers required.

The word 'volunteer' can mean several things in archaeology. Some excavations, particularly meagrely financed research digs, seek genuine, unpaid volunteers, though they may be provided with food and accommodation. Alternatively, 'volunteers' on government or local authority funded rescue projects may be paid a small amount to cover living expenses. The advantage of the research excavation is that often the setting is attractive, it is usually carried out in the summer, the volunteers come together for a particular short period, and there can be a lot of enthusiasm. On the other hand, the best 'rescue' excavations also have valid and interesting 'research' priorities. They should be planned well in advance of or phased in with the redevelopment programme so that the work is not a last-minute scramble. Rescue excavations are not confined to the summer vacation season, and if a wind-swept gravel pit in November does not seem immediately attractive, it at least means that there are opportunities to join excavations throughout the year.

Most large rescue projects are financed by the Department of the Environment's Directorate of Ancient Monuments and Historic Buildings. The Directorate maintains a central archaeological unit whose job it is to carry out excavations, but the majority of the work is financed indirectly. Grants are

given to local or regional archaeological committees who then organize excavation units to carry out the work in their own area. Archaeological units are to be found in major historic towns such as York and Lincoln; others work principally within a county; and some are regional, covering up to three counties. Recently the trend has been towards the last of these. It has been said that British archaeology has more organizations than organization, and the clearest guide through the present confused structure is undoubtedly John Bishop's excellent booklet *Opportunities for Archaeologists*.

Archaeological units, in contrast with archaeological societies, are professional organizations carrying out surveys and excavations sponsored by the Department of the Environment and often local authorities and universities as well. This is not to say that they do not welcome help from interested amateur archaeologists. The links between units and societies are usually very close, and volunteers are welcome on most sites. The role of non-professionals is particularly relevant nowadays as there is a growing tendency for the Department of the Environment to finance only larger excavation projects. This means that many locally important sites may disappear unrecorded unless an active amateur group comes to the rescue.

One kind of participation which archaeologists do not welcome is the destructive digging of treasure-hunters armed with metal-detectors. The fundamental difference between archaeology and treasure-hunting is that while the purpose of the former is to recover information about the past the latter is directed principally by the hope of personal gain. Archaeologists themselves rarely use metal-detectors as they are of limited value in serious research work. This is mainly because to an archaeologist the value of an object as evidence lies principally in its context—exactly where it is in the ground in relation to the surrounding stratigraphy. The treasure-hunter who removes a Roman coin from a site may have obtained an interesting curio worth a few pounds but he has destroyed most of its historic value.

Metal-detectors are being promoted by commercial firms on a large scale. Their leaflets, explicitly or implicitly, even encourage treasure-hunters to break the law by raking through scheduled ancient monuments. As an activity this is about as useful as picking rare flowers in a botanical garden or stealing osprey eggs. The attraction of finding unusual objects, antiquities or even striking it rich is an obvious one, but metal-detectors should be used only where they can result in the minimum amount of damage, such as on beaches or stream beds. Anyone with a serious interest in the past would do much better to join an archaeological society.

Many people are first introduced to archaeology through evening classes organized by the Workers' Education Association (WEA) or a university extra-mural department. Archaeology is one of the fastest-growing subjects in the field of adult education—over 40,000 students attended courses in Britain in 1976. Certain extra-mural departments are strong in the subject, notably Birmingham, Bristol, Leicester and Oxford, but there are several

others providing a wide range of courses for all levels of interest, from day-schools to three-year courses leading to a certificate in archaeology. Most departments publish their syllabuses in September, and it is well worth checking the local library or the nearest extra-mural department to see what is available.

Evening classes are tending to become less passive, and many students now become involved in original work. In 1977 the first archaeology prize sponsored by Rescue, *Current Archaeology* and the BBC was won by a group of students from Manchester University's Extra-Mural Department for their fieldwork on Offa's Dyke. Quite a few people have, in fact, gone on to become full-time archaeologists as a result of catching the bug while perched behind the all-too-common miniature desk in the village schoolroom.

Talking of schoolrooms, archaeology is only rarely taught there during the daytime. More and more teachers are becoming aware of the possibilities of archaeology as a vivid aspect of historical and environmental studies, but only about 100 pupils a year take any formal examination in the subject. This may be partly due to the excessive difficulty of the 'A' level syllabus. Many museums and their education departments are now gearing their activities and displays more towards schoolchildren. Rescue, the trust for British Archaeology, is very active in this area, and Young Rescue, with branches around the country, aims to involve young people in archaeological work. The CBA is also attempting to encourage the development of archaeology in schools.

Some archaeological units have arrangements with local schools so that groups of older students help on excavations. Because of insurance regulations children usually have to be over fourteen years of age, though younger individuals can sometimes be found interesting work to do. Teachers should remember, though, that excavation itself is a strenuous job, requiring skill and patience, and is not a suitable activity for most people below the fourth or fifth form in secondary schools. Nevertheless, the immediacy of archaeology and the historical interest of the landscape around us make it in many ways an ideal subject to teach in schools. Young people who wish to find out about university courses and job prospects should start by reading John Bishop's *Opportunities for Archaeologists*. Those who actually intend to study archaeology at university would benefit greatly by spending a year working with an archaeological organization before starting their course.

Archaeology, at its best, is a participant sport, but the interested armchair observer will find no shortage of books, covering all aspects of the subject. The short bibliography at the end of this book indicates just a few of the more useful ones for the recent convert.

The annual journals of the county archaeological societies are the traditional medium for the publication of academic articles. They vary tremendously in quality and the regularity of their appearance. Some seem disconcertingly like their nineteenth-century forebears, while others are up-to-date and relatively

cheap, as many of their articles (the ones publishing the results of rescue excavation) are heavily subsidized by the Department of the Environment. Annual journals are also produced by such august national bodies as the Prehistoric Society and the Society of Antiquaries.

At a more popular level the best-known periodical is *Current Archaeology*, appearing up to six times a year. It contains well-illustrated accounts of recent excavations in Britain as well as reviews, letters and a job-finder section. The quarterly *Antiquity* does not restrict itself to the British Isles. Although less attractively produced than *Current Archaeology*, *Antiquity* covers a wider variety of subjects and is spiced by the editorials of Glyn Daniel. There is, perhaps surprisingly, no really commercial, mass-circulation magazine on archaeology in Britain. Unfortunately, this gap is being filled by the treasure-hunting press and the lunatic fringe. Any book that contains photographs of Easter Island statues, pyramids, South American ruins and phrases like 'How could primitive man possibly . . .?' should be assumed, in the first instance, to be low-grade and irrational science fiction.

Archaeology's widest audience is probably gained through television. If the younger generation do not quite live up to the erudite, eccentric and theatrical image of Sir Mortimer Wheeler and his colleagues on *Animal, Vegetable and Mineral* in the 50s, programmes like *Chronicle* present lively and interesting accounts of archaeological subjects. In 1977 BBC Radio formed a permanent archaeological unit in Bristol to collect information and organize regular programmes.

The work of archaeologists should ultimately be on show in a museum. The museum's role is to collect, preserve, display and make available for study the material evidence of the past. Many people will come into contact with archaeology for the first time in a museum. If it is a dusty, dreary, 'dingy municipal repository', it may well be the last time. Fortunately, many of them now employ designers to create attractive displays. The national mega-museums like the British Museum can be overpowering if swallowed whole. It is sensible to take them a little at a time: spend an hour at the magnificent display of the Sutton Hoo ship burial or introduce yourself to the statue of Idrimi, King of Alalakh in Syria 3,500 years ago. In small doses a large museum can be a pleasure for years; too much, and you are likely to catch a debilitating dose of cultural indigestion.

Some of the most imaginative and popular museums are the relatively new outdoor ones which attempt to involve the visitor. Ironbridge Museum in Shropshire concentrates on industrial archaeology; the Weald and Downland Museum, Singleton, in Sussex and Avoncroft, near Bromsgrove, have re-erected and reconstructed old buildings; while St Fagan's in Glamorgan re-creates Welsh folk-life.

It needs a great deal of historical imagination to imagine what a place might have looked like on the evidence of a scatter of post-holes and the rubbish of long-dead people. Drawings, such as those of Allen Sorrell, scale models or

life-size reconstruction are more than just a popular form of interpretation; they force an excavator to think hard about the details of a site and provide an answer to that most important but most difficult of questions 'But what did it look like?'

The ultimate in models can be seen at the Roman fort of the Lunt, Baginton, near Coventry. Coventry Museum recruited the help of twenty-five Royal Engineers to rebuild the gate of the fort in three days, followed later by part of the defences and one of the garrison's granaries. Excavation evidence was combined with other sources of information, such as the scenes on Trajan's Column, to produce as accurate a piece of work as possible. A similar exercise was carried out a few years ago at the Roman fort of Metchley in Birmingham. Unfortunately, it attracted the persistent attention of hostile Brummy tribesmen who burnt it down.

Unsuspecting drivers along the busy A3 near Petersfield in Hampshire may wonder at the thatched, African-style hut perched on the slopes of Butser Hill. This is the site of the most comprehensive programme of archaeological reconstruction and experimentation in Britain, the Butser Hill Experimental Iron Age Farm.

Experimental archaeology, or action archaeology as it is known in the United States, is the controlled reconstruction of structures, the utilization of ancient tools or the manufacture of ancient products in an attempt to see how things actually work. As well as building Iron Age-style houses based on excavation plans, Peter Reynolds, the project leader, and his helpers have collected together animals as similar to prehistoric ones as possible. Modern Soay sheep from St Kilda in the Hebrides are most like those kept on Iron Age farms; Dexter cattle, all-purpose family-sized beasts, approximate to the small prehistoric types; and a Tamworth sow has been encouraged to form a relationship with a European wild boar in order to create a new generation of Iron Age-style piglets. The Dexters are used to plough Celtic fields in which prehistoric cereals (emmer, einkorn and spelt) are grown, along with woad, Celtic beans and fat hen. The yields are monitored, and the grain stored in underground pits of the type common in Iron Age settlements. Perhaps surprisingly to most people the losses in these pits are fewer than in modern silos and they are completely pest-free. Happily, at Butser Hill they have recently built an annexe which is open to the public.

While open-air museums and experimental farms aim to put flesh on the bare bones of history, many people prefer to take their archaeology neat. The fascination of ruins can be experienced best at the many sites held in guardianship by the Department of the Environment. The Department has been particularly successful in preserving castles and monasteries, although other types of site have fared less well. The little blue booklets which describe the monuments are especially good value.

A very welcome development has been the entry of local authorities into the preservation of ancient remains. In some cases they may be incorporated

Butser Hill, Hampshire: a general view of the experimental Iron Age farm. Soay sheep graze in the nearer paddock, and two circular huts, based on excavation plans from Maiden Castle and Pimperne in Dorset, have been constructed.

Soay sheep.

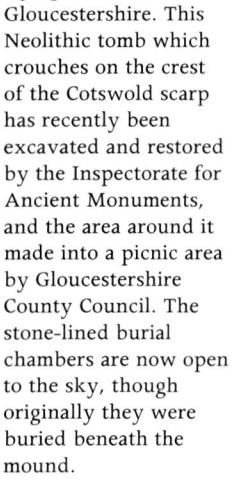

Nympsfield, Gloucestershire. This Neolithic tomb which crouches on the crest of the Cotswold scarp has recently been excavated and restored by the Inspectorate for Ancient Monuments, and the area around it made into a picnic area by Gloucestershire County Council. The stone-lined burial chambers are now open to the sky, though originally they were buried beneath the mound.

Threatened by its popularity—Badbury Rings, Dorset. This hill-fort is a horrifying example of bad land management. Thousands of visitors on foot, in cars and on motorcycles swarm over it wearing out the turf and exposing the chalk beneath which is rapidly eroded, creating disfiguring scars.

within a country park, such as the motte and bailey at Clare Castle in west Suffolk, or in a picnic area like the Neolithic tomb at Nympsfield in Gloucestershire. Others like the Palaeolithic caves at Cresswell Crags, run by Derbyshire and Nottinghamshire County Councils, have attractive visitor centres attached to them. Popularity brings problems, and thousands of feet can wreak havoc on the ramparts of a hill-fort like Badbury Rings in Dorset. At Danebury, in contrast, Hampshire County Council carefully manage the site so that it is not spoilt as a result of its own attractiveness.

Many county and district authorities now accept that they have a responsibility to their historic heritage. Essex County Council, a pioneer in this field, combines an enlightened policy of protection with booklets, such as its *Historic Features*, which are designed to encourage interest in the local landscape. This is conservation in its widest sense, including not only castles, villas and hillforts but also ancient woods, hedges and plants. Hatfield Forest, for example, in the words of John Hedges, the Essex County Archaeologist, 'warrants the same protection as a Grade 1 Listed Building' as it 'remains today almost exactly as a deer park would have looked in medieval times'.

Archaeology has come a long way since the days of the grog-swilling, barrow-digging men. Archaeologists now find themselves not only in their traditional bastions, the universities and museums, but also in county planning departments, computer centres and construction camps. But the professionals are only the tip of the iceberg—a mere 500 or so of them in the British Isles. The study of archaeology is becoming increasingly complex and specialized, but the interest it still arouses at the grass roots is, as I said at the beginning of this book, one of its great strengths. The past is all around us and belongs to everyone. The study of the past is not a retreat into nostalgia; it is an attempt to understand ourselves.

Bibliography

CHAPTER 1
Daniel, G., *150 Years of Archaeology*, London, 1975
Piggott, S., *Ruins in a Landscape: Essays in Antiquarianism*, Edinburgh, 1976

CHAPTER 2
Daniel, G., *The Idea of Prehistory*, London, 1962
Fleming, S., *Dating in Archaeology: A Guide to Scientific Techniques*, London, 1976
Renfrew, C., *Before Civilisation: Radiocarbon Revolution and Prehistoric Europe*,
    London, 1973
Renfrew, C. (Ed.), *British Prehistory, a New Outline*, London, 1974

CHAPTER 3
Aston, M. A. and Rowley, R. T., *Landscape Archaeology: An Introduction to
    Fieldwork Techniques on Post-Roman Landscapes*, Newton Abbot, 1974
Evans, J. G., *The Environment of Early Man in the British Isles*, London, 1975
Fowler, P. J. (Ed.), *Recent Work in Rural Archaeology*, Bradford on Avon, 1975
Hoskins, W. G., *The Making of the English Landscape*, 2nd. ed., London, 1977
Taylor, C., *Fieldwork in Mediaeval Archaeology*, London, 1974
Taylor, C., *Fields in the English Landscape*, London, 1975

CHAPTER 4
Aston, M. A. and Bond, J., *The Landscape of Towns*, London, 1976
Brunskill, R. W., *Illustrated Handbook of Vernacular Architecture*, London, 1970
Platt, C. P. S., *The English Medieval Town*, London, 1976

CHAPTER 5
Dymond, D. P., *Archaeology and History: A Plea for Reconciliation*, London, 1974
Thomas, D. H., *Predicting the Past: An Introduction to Anthropological Archaeology*,
    New York, 1974

CHAPTER 7
Barker, P. A., *Techniques of Excavation*, London, 1977
Bishop, J., *Opportunities for Archaeologists* (Rescue Publication No. 5), Hertford,
    1975
Coles, J. M., *Archaeology by Experiment*, London, 1973
Rahtz, P. A. (Ed.), *Rescue Archaeology*, Harmondsworth, 1974
Webster, G., *Practical Archaeology: An Introduction to Archaeological Fieldwork
    and Excavation*, London, 1963

Index

Page numbers in italic indicate illustrations.

An Introduction to

Archaeology